INTERNATIONAL LIGHT CUISINE

Chris Borges

with nutritional analysis by
Bonnie Hechtkopf, M.S., R.D., L.D.

Dedication

To my husband, Fernando, for being my guiding light in our quest to prepare delicious and healthy meals. It is with great love and affection that I treasure our time together — in and out of the kitchen. To my sons, John and Paul, for being wonderfully receptive to all of my creations! To my mother and father, Carole and John Walker for the encouragement they've always given me.

Library of Congress Catalog Card Number 93-78613
ISBN 0-9633070-2-9

For additional information, contact:

GemServ, Inc.

10460 Roosevelt Boulevard, Suite 248
St. Petersburg, FL 33716-3818
813/572-6933

Published in the U.S.A.

Acknowledgements

Writing a book isn't something you do on your own. It takes a tremendous team effort to put it all together. So many people gave of their time, friendship and energy to help me complete *International Light Cuisine*.

First of all, many thanks to my family — Fernando, John and Paul — for being so patient while I experimented with recipes and wrote for countless hours, even on family vacations. I could have never fulfilled my dream without their love and support. My mother, Carole Walker, deserves a special medal for listening to and encouraging my ideas. I only wish my Dad could have been here to see his favorite recipes in writing.

I owe a great deal to my publisher, Deborah Kenly, who is truly responsible for orchestrating the entire book. From our first meeting, to the day we gave it a name, to the final hour of completion, Deborah was there. I thank you for being a great publisher and for becoming a good friend.

To Betty Sembler, who introduced me to Deborah Kenly when I was looking for a publisher. Thank you for being so loving and supportive. • To Bonnie Hechtkopf, who, as a licensed dietitian, spent countless hours analyzing each and every recipe in this book. • To Bruce Evensen of Thomas Bruce Photography, whose unique ability speaks for itself. I really appreciate your patience and professionalism. • To Marjorie Kane, our professional food stylist, whose talent with artistic food presentation made the photography come to life. • To Ralph Campanella, for planting the beautiful garden from where I pick the herbs for my recipes. Thanks to Ralph, fresh herbs are as close as my own backyard. • To Pam Hinds of Special Secretarial Services, who was always good natured and willing to drop everything to help me. • To Tyler Krieble, who filled in the gaps of my beverage recommendations by providing his expertise on beer. • To the entire editing and production staff who worked tirelessly to make each recipe comprehensive and the format easy to follow.

The support of my family and friends has been overwhelming — perhaps that's why they all have an open invitation to dinner.

Foreword

You might wonder why I would take the time to write a cookbook. After all, there are thousands of cookbooks on the market and, with society going in the direction of shortcut meals, it *is* easy to ask, "Why do we need another one?"

The cuisine we consume is a melting pot of flavors introduced by our ancestors. I think it's about time someone updated these old favorites. It's for just this reason that I've spent countless hours creating, testing, cooking and writing to come up with this book about international cuisine — with special emphasis on lowfat preparation techniques. I think it's unreasonable to believe that people have hours at their disposal to prepare healthy, home-cooked meals on a regular basis. My goal is to educate you on how to have fun preparing good food *that's good for you* in a short period of time.

Every evening should be a special occasion. Granted, it isn't always easy to be elegant on a Tuesday night when you've had to work late and the threat of homework looms on the horizon. But believe me, with a little practice it can be done. It takes no more time to prepare a lovely pasta than it does to drive through the local fast food restaurant. The key is organization!

The dinner hour is generally your one and only time to sit down in a relaxed atmosphere. If there is only one thing to be learned from the European lifestyle, it is to master their way of enjoying food. Each meal is a celebration in its own right — even a simple broiled chicken dinner is presented with finesse.

The food I prepare during the week is generally pretty simple, taking no more than an hour or so in the kitchen. Most recipes in this book can be prepared with ease. Add a salad and bread and you have a healthy "fast food" dinner. It's enough to put anyone in a better frame of mind to tackle homework or other evening tasks.

So, that's why I wrote *International Light Cuisine*. It's my chance to share with you what's worked so well for me all these years.

Your partner in healthy cooking,

Chris Borges

TABLE OF CONTENTS

NUTRITIONAL ANALYSIS

Your quick and easy guide to understanding the basics

As a registered dietitian, my role in *International Light Cuisine* was to analyze the recipes. The computer software I used was DINE Right for Windows*. Other programs on the market may yield different results. The DINE Right database contains over 5,600 foods including a large range of brand name, ethnic and fast foods. Additional items were added to the database through consultation with food manufacturers and supermarket research of hot new items. Many new "fat-free" or "reduced fat" foods were used in the compilation of this cookbook. The marketplace is turning out more and more of them every day. They can be used very successfully to reduce the fat in otherwise high-fat favorites. Keep in mind that these calculated values are approximations only. All of the numbers have been rounded off for the sake of simplicity and convenience. Unless an item is specifically listed as an ingredient, the analysis does not include it. This is most relevant with both seasonings and garnishes, especially salt.

ILC is a great choice for your kitchen library. It is appealing in its huge array of ethnic and regional adaptations. There are many succulent vegetarian recipes to tempt us as we try to follow the new USDA Food Guide Pyramid and cut back on meat, poultry and fish. The desserts are fabulous and surprisingly low in fat. We can assemble entire menus from this book or just incorporate one or two recipes into our meals. Pick and choose keeping in mind that these recipes are designed to be part of a well-balanced diet.

In the 1990's we are focused on several health-oriented issues. Cutting back on our fat intake towards a goal of 30 percent or less of total calories per day is critical. Reducing cholesterol to 300 milligrams (mg) per day is also wise. *ILC* will help you to accomplish these goals. Remember, the key to lowering cholesterol is to decrease not only the cholesterol in a given food but also the total fat in your diet, especially saturated fat. We have also come to realize that reliance on salt as a seasoning is not only unhealthy but boring. Limiting sodium intake to somewhere between 2,000 to 3,000 mg is desirable. If this is your concern, consider eliminating or cutting back on some of the foods higher in sodium such as olives, capers, canned broth, shellfish and cheese. Chris has utilized a whole array of different herbs, spices and sauces to perk up your taste buds and set you on a healthier course.

Primarily, olive oil was used in the recipes, except for the occasional vegetable shortening needed for baking. The most up-to-date scientific research indicates that olive oil, which is monounsaturated, does not increase the risk of either cancer or heart disease. If you do not like the flavor, you might want to try canola oil as an alternative. Both olive oil and canola oil are considered the top choices by today's health experts. Whichever you choose, remember that they contain 13 grams (g) of total fat and 120 calories per tablespoon. Today, even non-stick cooking sprays aren't just for greasing pans anymore. Use them as part of your cooking process as well.

* For more information on DINE Right for Windows, contact DINE Systems, Inc., 586 N. French Road, Amherst, NY 14228. (716) 688-2492.

NUTRITIONAL ANALYSIS

Finally, a review of how to compute the fat in your diet may be helpful to you. Using a 2,000 calorie diet as an example, you can figure out what the current guidelines are recommending. If you are consuming 2,000 calories per day, you want to limit fat to 30 percent. This would allow you 600 calories for the total daily fat in your food. To figure out how many grams of fat this is, divide 600 by 9 (since there are 9 calories in each gram of fat). In this example, we get 67 g of fat per day. To further illustrate, if you are serving a meat-based entrée whose fat is more than 30 percent of total calories, make sure to balance it with vegetables, fruits and grain products so that you will attain your overall goal of 30 percent fat for the day. You should adjust this figure according to your own caloric needs.

Although *ILC* was designed to be a healthy cookbook, if you have more specific medical or nutritional needs, you should regard the analysis section as simply a guideline. Chris's objective was to create recipes that are lower in fat, sodium and cholesterol than the more traditional presentations. Impressively, lowfat here does *not* mean low taste.

Bonnie Hechtkopf, M.S., R.D., L.D.
Consulting dietitian in St. Petersburg, Florida

NUTRITIONAL GUIDELINES AT A GLANCE

Fat	*no more than 30% of total calories*
Sodium	*2,000 to 3,000 mg per day*
Cholesterol	*no more than 300 mg per day*

Increase your intake of complex carbohydrate foods by eating more bread, dry beans, rice, corn, barley, rye, oats, wheat, pasta, fruits and vegetables.

FUNDAMENTALS

Guidelines on the philosophy of International Light Cuisine

Portion Sizes • In calculating the nutritional analysis, many of the portion sizes may seem smaller than what you are accustomed to. For instance, 3 ounces of meat or a 2-inch square brownie might look a little skimpy. However, in my overall planning, I also allow for a starch, vegetable and often a salad that rounds out the caloric content of the meal. Your family may eat differently, so adapt the recipes according to your own personal style. My philosophy about creating healthy menus involves the overall inclusion of fats, proteins, carbohydrates, etc. We certainly *could* eat more, but why *should* we?

Prep/Cook Times • Preparation and cooking times are simply an approximation. As you become more familiar with the recipes and adapt them to your particular style, these times may increase or decrease. Cooking times can also vary greatly depending on your type of oven, stove or grill. Additionally, other factors can alter your results including altitude and humidity. Use these recommendations as a guide only, but allow enough time to make any necessary adjustments.

Many recipes are accompanied by rice or pasta. These cooking times (rice 20 minutes, pasta 12 minutes) may often be prepared concurrently to cut down on your overall cooking time. Remember that it also takes approximately 5 minutes for the water to boil. Simply coordinate these items during the latter part of the cooking process.

When sautéing garlic and onion in olive oil, pay close attention so that theydon't burn. Sautéing until golden is a good rule of thumb. Remember, they will continue to cook when the balance of the ingredients are added.

Seafood • Seafood is naturally high in sodium although these recipes are lighter versions than you would ordinarily find.

While I prefer to use raw crawfish, they're not always easy to find. Cooking times in the book are based on using raw crawfish. If using the pre-cooked fresh or frozen variety, reduce the cooking time by approximately 5 to 8 minutes.

Seasonings/Garnishes • Unless a measurement of salt and pepper are listed in the ingredients, they have not been included in the analysis. Garnishes are also not figured in. Keep in mind that any additional seasonings used may change the nutritional values.

Food Processor • All recipes that call for a food processor should be used with the knife blade. If you do not own a food processor, purée with a blender instead. For chopping and mincing, substitute a sharp knife and cutting board.

FUNDAMENTALS

Beverage Selections • In each chapter, I've mentioned only a few of the more popular selections of wine, beer and coffee based on my personal taste. These complement the dishes featured but, by no means, provide a comprehensive accounting of the choices you have available to you. As a guideline, I suggest only general categories which may be served with particular courses.

Like wine, beer is grouped according to ingredients and personal taste. They fall into 3 categories: Lagers, Wheat Beers and a group containing Ales. When choosing a beer to enjoy with your meal, one brewed in the country of origin will typically be the best match for the particular styles listed.

> Lagers • Pilsners (typical of most American beers), Amber Lagers, Bocks
> Wheat Beers • Lambics, Weisses (flavored syrups may be added)
> Ales • Mild Ales, Pale Ales, Porters

Brand Information • Absolutely no endorsements are intended by listing these products below. They are simply included to inform you of which brands were used by our licensed dietician in calculating the nutritional values. You, of course, may use any brands you prefer with the knowledge that there may be some possible changes in the nutritional content.

Hot pepper sauce	Tabasco	Nonfat whipped topping	Cool Whip Lite
Egg product	Egg Beaters	Non-stick cooking spray	Pam
Vegetable shortening	Crisco	Worcestershire sauce	Lea & Perrins

Whenever lowfat milk was called for in a recipe, 1% lowfat milk was used. You may substitute skim milk to further reduce the fat content.

MEASUREMENT EQUIVALENTS

1 tablespoon = 3 teaspoons
2 tablespoons = 1 ounce
4 tablespoons = $\frac{1}{4}$ cup
5$\frac{1}{3}$ tablespoons = $\frac{1}{3}$ cup
8 tablespoons = $\frac{1}{2}$ cup
12 tablespoons = $\frac{3}{4}$ cup
16 tablespoons = 1 cup
1 cup = 8 ounces or $\frac{1}{2}$ pint
4 cups = 1 quart
4 quarts = 1 gallon

1 6$\frac{1}{2}$ to 8-ounce can = 1 cup
1 10$\frac{1}{2}$ to 12-ounce can = 1$\frac{1}{2}$ cups
1 14 to 16-ounce can = 1$\frac{3}{4}$ cups
1 16 to 17-ounce can = 2 cups
1 18 to 20-ounce can = 2$\frac{1}{2}$ cups
1 29-ounce can = 3$\frac{1}{2}$ cups
1 46 to 51-ounce can = 5$\frac{3}{4}$ cups
1 6$\frac{1}{2}$ to 7$\frac{1}{2}$-pound can or
number 10 = 12 to 13 cups

METRIC

Liquid
1 teaspoon = 5 milliliters
1 tablespoon = 15 milliliters
1 fluid ounce = 30 milliliters
1 cup = 250 milliliters
1 pint = 500 milliliters

Dry
1 quart = 1 liter
1 ounce = 30 grams
1 pound = 450 grams
2.2 pounds = 1 kilogram

HELPFUL HINTS

Suggestions for a healthier, happier time in the kitchen

Here are a few tricks that I've found helpful over the years...

- Prepare ingredients as much as possible before cooking. You'll have more time to be creative if you don't have to cut up vegetables at the last minute.
- Prepare and store foods ahead of time whenever possible. Quite often they taste better the next day anyway.
- Make sure to wash cutting boards thoroughly after cutting raw poultry. Bacteria can settle in before you know it.
- Never use poultry shears to cut anything but poultry.
- Keep carving knives well sharpened and in their block or rack when not in use.
- Wine is used in many of these recipes. If it's not your preference, simply cut back or eliminate it altogether by substituting broth, water or juice.
- Garlic cloves are easily peeled by lightly tapping them with a meat pounder or pressing the clove carefully with the flat side of the blade of a large knife.
- Be extra careful not to overcook seafood. It can become dry and tough. Follow the approximated cooking times and watch closely to see when the shrimp turn pink or the clams and mussels open.
- Don't wash mushrooms. They tend to hold water and become spongy. Instead, wipe them well with a moist paper towel to properly clean them.
- Squeeze fresh lemon juice on cooked vegetables instead of settling for rich sauces.
- Fresh fruit and sorbets are refreshing finales — skip the fat-laden desserts.
- Have confidence in your cooking. Anybody can fix wonderful, healthy meals that don't take all day. Practice on your family and you'll be ready for the talk-show circuit in no time!

Washing Seafood • While it is important to clean shellfish properly, it is also important not to remove the flavor of the sea.

Shrimp • To wash shrimp, rinse with cold water *before* peeling to remove any sand or foreign particles. Peel and remove the vein but do not wash again as the water will leave the shrimp tasting bland.

Squid • Rinse squid briefly to remove sand or foreign particles. All cartilage should be removed by pulling it loose with your fingers.

Mussels/Clams • Scrub shells thoroughly with a brush and water to remove foreign bodies. If they appear very sandy, soak them, uncooked, in cold water for 30 minutes.

HELPFUL HINTS

Crawfish • Crawfish are similar to lobsters in appearance. Since they are small, it takes patience to clean the heads and remove the meat from the tails. To separate, hold the crawfish right-side-up firmly with one hand and move the tail end back and forth with your other hand to "crack" it apart. It takes practice, but soon they'll come apart easily. To clean and prepare the heads for stuffing, use a small pick to remove the contents carefully, leaving the shell intact. Nothing here is edible, so throw it away. Rinse the head under running water and drain on paper towels. The tail meat can be removed by flipping the tail over and either running a knife down the soft side of the middle or cracking it open with your hands. Again, this takes a little work. Experiment to find a way that's most comfortable for you.

Baking • It is very important not to overwork the pastry dough. Mix only as much dough as is necessary and keep the mixture cool. Add as little water as possible. This helps to ensure a flaky pie crust.

Food Storage • Proper storage of food is an integral part of cooking. Since you should always buy the freshest ingredients possible, storing them properly not only prevents spoilage but preserves taste.

If you have an herb garden, fresh herbs should be cut at the time you need them. If you purchase these herbs from a produce market, wrap them in a damp paper towel, put them in a plastic storage bag and into the refrigerator until ready for use.

Vegetables should be stored in the refrigerator if they are not going to be consumed within 24 hours. Simply place them in plastic storage bags and into the vegetable crisper. Fruit may sit out at room temperature until it ripens. At that point, placing it in the refrigerator, uncovered, can slow down the ripening process.

Always store fish, poultry and meat in the refrigerator or freezer. It's best to thaw them in the refrigerator rather than at room temperature to prevent bacteria from growing. Never leave a stuffed turkey sitting at room temperature for longer than the duration of the meal. Remove all stuffing to a serving bowl. Once the meal has ended, remove the meat from the carcass, cover and refrigerate or freeze. Discard the carcass.

Eating at Restaurants • Don't sacrifice healthy eating habits to enjoy a night out. Many ingredients you see in restaurants are a bit on the high-fat side — with butter and creamy sauces. Review the menu and, if there is an item you'd like to try, ask your server to request that the chef prepare it in a lighter manner. A small amount of olive oil can be substituted for butter and an herb-wine sauce for its creamy counterpart. You won't miss the flavor or deviate from your overall healthy eating habits.

GLOSSARY

al dente • Literally means "to the tooth." Cooking pasta and vegetables to the point where they still are a little crunchy when bitten into.

à la mode • A dessert served with a small scoop of ice cream or frozen yogurt.

Bake • A method of cooking by dry heat in an oven or over hot coals.

Baklava • A Greek baked dessert of very thin sheets of pastry layered with nuts and honey or sugar syrup.

Baste • To moisten with pan drippings, sauce, etc. during cooking time.

Beat • To mix foods vigorously and thoroughly with a spoon, fork or electric mixer.

Blanch • To immerse, usually vegetables or fruit, briefly into boiling water to inactivate enzymes, loosen skin or remove excess salt.

Blend • To combine ingredients, of which at least one is liquid or soft, to uniform consistency.

Boil • To heat liquid until rapidly bubbling.

Braise • To cook, especially meats, covered, in a small amount of liquid.

Broil • To cook by direct exposure to intense heat such as a flame or an electric heating unit.

Butterfly • To split almost in half, leaving enough flesh intact to keep the food whole.

Caramelize • To heat sugar in a skillet, stirring constantly, until melted and golden brown.

Chill • To cool completely in the refrigerator or in cracked ice before serving.

Cobbler • A deep-dish fruit pie made with pastry or biscuit dough on top.

Cocoa • Powdered form of unsweetened chocolate from which cocoa butter has been removed.

Crêpe • A small thin pancake filled with fruit or filling, rolled or folded around its contents.

Crush • The process of using a spoon or fork to break a whole piece into a smaller piece without actually cutting it.

Custard • A smooth pudding that is a mixture of eggs, milk and sugar, baked until set.

Cut in • To disperse solid shortening into dry ingredients with a knife or pastry cutter. Texture of the mixture should resemble coarse cracker meal.

Deglaze • To heat stock, wine or other liquid in the pan in which meat has been cooked, mixing with pan juices to form a gravy or sauce base.

Degrease • To remove accumulated fat from the surface of hot liquids.

Dice • To cut into very small cubes between 1/8 and 1/4 inch.

Dissolve • To thoroughly mix a solid or granular substance with a liquid until no sediment remains.

Dredge • To coat completely with eggs, flour, bread crumbs, etc.

Filet • To remove bones from meat or fish. Pieces of meat, fish or poultry from which bones have been removed are called filets.

Flambé • The process of adding liquor to food and igniting it to produce a flaming effect.

Flan • An egg custard glazed with caramel or fruit.

Flute • To make a decorative scalloped border around the edge of a pie or tart crust.

Fold in • To blend a delicate, frothy mixture into a heavier one preferably with a rubber spatula so that none of the lightness or volume is lost. The motion used is one of turning under and bringing up and over, rotating the bowl 1/4 turn as you go.

Glaze • To coat with sauce, egg white or a jellied substance to add firmness, color and flavor.

Grate • To rub food against a rough, perforated utensil to produce slivers, chunks, curls, etc.

GLOSSARY

Grill • To broil, usually over hot coals or gas.

Grind • To cut, crush or force through a chopper to produce small bits.

Julienne • To cut fruits and vegetables into long thin strips for use in salads and garnishes.

Knead • To press, fold and stretch dough until smooth and elastic.

Marinate • The process of soaking food in a specific liquid to tenderize it or give it a special flavor.

Melt • To liquefy solid foods by heating.

Meringue • A dessert topping baked from a mixture of stiffly beaten egg whites and sugar.

Mince • To chop foods into very small pieces.

Mix • To combine ingredients by stirring or beating to distribute them uniformly.

Mold • To shape into a particular form.

Mousse • A sweetened chilled or frozen dessert made with flavored whipped cream or egg whites.

Parboil • To partially cook in boiling water.

Pit • To remove the inedible seed from fruit, etc.

Plump • To soak fruits, usually dried, in liquid until puffy and softened. Can also refer to chicken.

Poach • To cook in simmering liquid.

Purée • To blend or strain until smooth and thick.

Reduce • To boil stock, gravy or other liquid until volume is lessened and liquid thickened.

Roast • To cook by dry heat either in an oven or over hot coals, especially with meat.

Roux • Flour and oil cooked together slowly, used as a thickening agent in soups and sauces.

Sauté • To cook, stirring frequently, in a small amount of oil or non-stick cooking spray.

Scald • To heat a liquid, such as milk, almost to the boiling point.

Sear • To cook meat at a very high temperature quickly on both sides to retain the juices.

Shortcake • A baked biscuit, cake or cookie which has been split, filled and topped with fruit, ice cream, frozen yogurt or whipped cream.

Shred • To cut or shave food into slivers.

Sieve • To press a mixture through a closely meshed utensil to make it uniform.

Sift • Putting flour or other dry ingredients through a sieve to obtain a finer, lighter consistency.

Simmer • To cook very slowly in liquid that is just below the boiling point.

Skewer • To thread foods onto a rod or to fasten the opening of stuffed fowl with small pins.

Sorbet • A fruit-flavored ice typically served between courses as a palate refresher. Also, sherbet made without milk.

Soufflé • A light airy dessert made most frequently with fruit or chocolate.

Steam • To cook with water vapor in a closed container — steamer, rack or double boiler.

Stew • To simmer, usually meats and vegetables, for a long period of time to tenderize.

Stock • Liquid formed by cooking poultry or meat with or without seasonings in water.

Strain • To pass through a strainer, sieve or cheesecloth to remove solids or impurities.

Tart • A small, open-faced pastry consisting of a shell filled with fruit, jam or custard.

Toss • To mix lightly with a lifting motion using two forks or spoons.

Truss • To bind poultry legs and wings close to the body before cooking.

Whip • To beat until light, airy and frothy.

Zest • The fine grating of the colored outermost coatings of citrus fruits.

Zester • The tool which easily removes the zest from citrus fruits.

SUBSTITUTIONS

Instead of   *Use*

BAKING

1 teaspoon baking powder .... ¼ teaspoon baking soda plus ½ teaspoon cream of tartar

1 tablespoon cornstarch .... 2 tablespoons all-purpose flour or 1 tablespoon tapioca

1 cup sifted all-purpose flour .... 1 cup plus 2 tablespoons sifted cake flour

1 cup sifted cake flour .... 1 cup minus 2 tablespoons sifted all-purpose flour

1 cup dry bread crumb .... ¾ cup cracker crumbs

DAIRY

1 whole egg .... 2 egg whites or ¼ cup egg product

1 cup buttermilk .... 1 cup sour milk or 1 cup yogurt

SEASONING

1 teaspoon allspice .... ½ teaspoon cinnamon plus ⅛ teaspoon cloves

1 cup catsup .... 1 cup tomato sauce plus ½ cup sugar
                                                    plus 2 tablespoons vinegar

1 garlic clove .... ⅛ teaspoon garlic powder or ⅛ teaspoon instant minced
                                                    garlic or ¾ teaspoon garlic salt or 5 drops of liquid garlic

1 teaspoon lemon juice .... ½ teaspoon vinegar

1 tablespoon mustard .... 1 teaspoon dry mustard

1 medium onion .... 1 tablespoon dried minced onion
                                                    or 1 teaspoon onion powder

SWEET

1 one-ounce square chocolate .... ¼ cup cocoa plus 1 teaspoon shortening

1⅔ ounces semisweet chocolate .... 1 ounce unsweetened chocolate plus 4 teaspoons
                                                    granulated sugar

1 cup honey .... 1 to 1¼ cups sugar plus ¼ cup liquid or 1 cup
                                                    corn syrup or molasses

1 cup granulated sugar .... 1 cup packed brown sugar or 1 cup corn syrup,
                                                    molasses or honey minus ¼ cup liquid

PACKAGING TERMS

Diet • Contains no more than 40 calories per serving. Also may have at least $\frac{1}{3}$ fewer calories than the product it replaces or resembles.

Extra lean • Denotes meat and poultry products that have no more than 5% fat by weight.

Lean • On meat and poultry products, indicates no more than 10% fat by weight. "Lean" may also be used as part of a brand name with no restriction other than it must have a nutritional label.

Leaner • Used on meat and poultry products with 25% less fat than the standard product. Does not necessarily mean that the product is low in fat.

Low calorie • Denotes products with no more than 40 calories per serving or 0.4 calories per gram of food.

Reduced calorie • Must contain at least $\frac{1}{3}$ fewer calories than the product it replaces or resembles. Label must show a comparison between the two.

Sugar free • Does not contain sucrose (table sugar) but may contain additional sweeteners such as honey, molasses or fructose, all of which increase the total calories.

Naturally sweetened • Food sweetened with a fruit or juice rather than sugar. There is no regulation on this term, however, so a naturally sweetened product can contain sugar or other refined sweeteners such as high-fructose corn sweetener.

No salt added/unsalted/without added salt • These terms mean no salt was added during processing, but the product may still have high sodium levels due to the use of other sodium-containing ingredients such as sodium phosphate, monosodium glutamate or baking powder.

Sodium free • Contains fewer than 5 milligrams of sodium per serving.

Reduced sodium • Reduced by at least 75% from usual level of sodium per serving.

Low sodium • No more than 140 mg of sodium per serving.

Very low sodium • 35 or fewer mg per serving.

Natural • Regarding meat and poultry, indicates the product contains no artificial flavors, colors, preservatives or synthetic ingredients. No legal definition exists for the "natural" in processed foods; e.g. natural potato chips, can have artificial colors or flavors added.

Naturally flavored • Flavoring must be from an extract, oil or derivative of a spice, herb, root, leaf or other natural source. Naturally flavored products can have artificial ingredients, however.

Organic • No legal definition exists. Use of the term is prohibited on meat and poultry.

No cholesterol • May not contain cholesterol but may contain large amounts of saturated fat such as coconut or palm oil, which tend to raise the level of cholesterol in the blood.

Saturated fats • Usually harden at room temperature. Found in animal and some vegetable products. Tend to raise cholesterol levels in the blood. Primarily in beef, veal, lamb, pork, ham, butter, cream, whole milk and regular cheeses. Saturated vegetable fats are found in solid and hydrogenated shortenings, coconut oil, cocoa butter, palm oil and palm kernel oil.

Hydrogenated fats • Fats and oils changed from their natural liquid form to become more solid, such as most margarine and shortening. May be partially or almost completely hydrogenated. Nutritionists generally advise us to avoid these since they resemble saturated fats.

CULINARY EQUIPMENT

Tools of the trade

The type of equipment you need in the kitchen depends on your level of cooking. I tend to use what I call "basic" cooking equipment nearly every day. Accordingly, I've taken inventory of my kitchen and have listed the things I couldn't live without. Since cooking is my passion, I am always adding some gadget or serving dish to my collection. One thing I always recommend is to invest in a sturdy set of cookware and good knives. You'll never regret it. They'll pay for themselves many times over in the long run. So build your own collection over time. There's no hurry — you don't have to spend a fortune to become a "great chef." Instead, plan for the future, invest in new "toys" wisely and enjoy the process of become more expert in affairs of the kitchen.

Appliances
Blender
Citrus juicer
Electric mixer
Food processor
Grill
Microwave

Bowls
Food storage containers
Mixing bowls in graduated sizes
Oven-proof glassware
Serving bowls
Wooden salad bowl

Measuring Devices
Measuring cups
Measuring spoons

Pots and Pans
Baking pans — large and small
Broiler pan
Cookie sheets
Large stockpot

Pie pan
Roasting pan
Saucepans — large and small
Sauté pans — large and small
Skillets — large and small
Springform pan

Utensils
Baster
Corkscrew
Knives — bread, paring, chef's, boning and sturdy rack or block with sharpening steel
Ladle
Long-handled cooking spoon
Long-handled slotted spoon
Mallet or pounder
Metal skewers
Metal tongs
Pasta tongs or server
Pastry brush
Pastry cutter
Potato masher

Poultry shears
Rolling pin
Spatulas — wooden, metal and rubber
Vegetable brush
Vegetable peeler
Wire whisk
Wooden spoons
Zester

Miscellaneous
Chopping board — wooden or plastic
Colanders — large and small
Grater
Salad spinner
Strainer or sieve
Vegetable steamer

Facing page — France (pictured clockwise): Chocolate Mousse, Mushroom and Leek Quiche, Salmon with Garlic and Herbs, Ratatouille, Niçoise Salad

Beverage Suggestions

WINE

Salad/Soup	• Chenin Blanc
	• Sauvignon Blanc
Poultry	• Red Burgundy
	• Red Bordeaux
Fish/Shellfish	• Chardonnay
	• Chablis
	• Sauvignon Blanc
	• White Burgundy
Quiche	• Beaujolais
Desserts	• Champagne

BEER

Light Soup/Quiche/Soufflé	• Pilsner
Poultry/Seafood	• Pilsner
	• Weisse
Vegetables	• Pilsner
Desserts	• Lambic
	• Weisse

COFFEE

Chocolate Raspberry
Espresso Roast
French Vanilla Cream
Rich French Roast

FRANCE

*L*et's unlock the mysteries of "Provincial cooking." It's not nearly as intimidating as you might imagine. When most people think of French food, they immediately picture Chicken Cordon Bleu, Poached Salmon with Béarnaise Sauce or a terrine of Pâté. When, in fact, Provincial cooking simply refers to cooking done in the individual provinces of France. It is, most of all, simple — allowing a piece of salmon or a plump chicken to taste its best without being smothered in rich cream sauces. In reality, most dishes produce their own juices anyway which eliminates the need for fattening extras. The recipes that follow are easily adapted to lowfat cooking methods.

There are eleven provinces of France, but in this chapter, we will focus on the lighter, healthier cuisine of Provence, located in Southeast France. Provence borders the Mediterranean Sea — source of the seafood that creates their famous fish soup, Bouillabaisse. The area also boasts the olive trees which give us their many fine olive oils. Additionally, a wide variety of fruits, vegetables, herbs and spices grow well in this region.

Different parts of Provence are impacted by other ethnic cuisines. For example, the eastern side is notably of Italian influence while the west picks up a more Spanish flavor. During my travels to France, I grew to appreciate all the provinces I was privileged to see. It was in Provence, however, where I felt most at home. The dishes there had already been prepared in a lowfat manner, without sacrificing any taste. Their philosophy was so similar to mine — the lighter the cooking process, the more natural the flavor.

FRANCE

SPICED TURKEY PÂTÉ

(Serves 6)

Prep Time: 35 minutes
Cook Time: 65 minutes
Misc Time: Chill 3 hours
           to overnight

Nutritional Analysis
per serving

Calories	227
Fat	7 g
Sodium	426 mg
Protein	25 g
Carbohydrates	6 g
Cholesterol	58 mg

1	pound freshly ground turkey breast
½	cup minced shallots
1	teaspoon minced garlic
2	tablespoons olive oil
⅓	cup Cognac
2	teaspoons lemon juice
1	teaspoon ground allspice
1	teaspoon salt
2	teaspoons ground white pepper
2	tablespoons all-purpose flour
¼	cup egg product
½	cup finely chopped parsley
	non-stick cooking spray
2	large bay leaves

Preheat oven to 350°. Place the turkey in a large bowl and set aside. In a skillet, sauté the shallots and garlic in the olive oil until golden. Add the Cognac. Cook over medium heat for 1 minute. Pour the mixture over the turkey. Add the lemon juice, allspice, salt, white pepper, flour, egg product and parsley. Mix thoroughly. Coat a small mold or terrine with the cooking spray. Spoon in the turkey mixture and smooth. Lay the bay leaves on top. Place foil snugly over the mold, and cover tightly with a lid. Place the mold inside a larger baking dish and pour water into the larger dish to reach halfway up the sides of the mold. Bake for 1 hour. Remove and loosely cover again with fresh foil and weight with a dish or other object. Cool. Chill, covered, for 3 hours to overnight. Discard the bay leaves. To serve, cut into slices from the mold or loosen the edges with a sharp knife. Invert onto a serving plate.

I like to serve molded Pâté with melba squares and tiny gherkins.

NIÇOISE SALAD

(Serves 6)

Salad:

1	large head Romaine lettuce
4	large ripe tomatoes, quartered
2	cups coarsely flaked tuna (freshly baked or canned in spring water)
12	Calamata olives, pitted
12	pieces canned white asparagus
½	cup thinly sliced red onion
1	cup ½-inch square French bread croutons vinaigrette dressing (see below)

Wash and dry the lettuce leaves well. Cut into small pieces and place in a large, fairly shallow salad bowl. Arrange the tomatoes, tuna, olives, asparagus and red onion on top of the lettuce.

Vinaigrette Dressing:

1	tablespoon olive oil
¼	cup red wine vinegar
2	tablespoons lemon juice
½	cup finely chopped parsley
2	tablespoons finely chopped chives

In a bowl or shaker bottle, combine all ingredients. Mix well. Pour over the salad. Toss lightly before serving.

Prep Time: 35 minutes

Nutritional Analysis per serving

Calories	172
Fat	6 g
Sodium	358 mg
Protein	13 g
Carbohydrates	12 g
Cholesterol	26 mg

BOUILLABAISSE
(Serves 10)

Prep Time: 1 hour
Cook Time: 2 hours

Nutritional Analysis
per serving

Calories	*603*
Fat	*13 g*
Sodium	*1121 mg*
Protein	*75 g*
Carbohydrates	*31 g*
Cholesterol	*205 mg*

Bouillon:

3	cups thinly sliced onion
4	teaspoons minced garlic
¼	cup olive oil
3	cups dry white wine
6	cups water
4	large fish heads
7	cups coarsely chopped tomatoes
2	teaspoons dried thyme
6	parsley sprigs
3	bay leaves
1	teaspoon crushed red pepper

In a large pot, sauté the onion and garlic in the olive oil until golden. Add the wine, water, fish heads, tomato, thyme, parsley, bay leaves and red pepper. Bring to a boil. Reduce heat and simmer, partially covered, for 35 minutes. Strain the bouillon through a large, fine sieve into another large stockpot. Be sure to press down hard against the fish heads and vegetables to extract their juices before discarding them.

Rouille:

2	small green bell peppers, seeded, diced
½	cup water
½	teaspoon crushed red pepper
½	cup dry white wine
½	cup coarsely chopped canned pimentos
3	garlic cloves, minced
2	tablespoons olive oil
¼	cup fine bread crumbs

In a saucepan, simmer the green pepper in water for approximately 10 minutes or until tender. Drain and dry thoroughly. In a food processor, blend the green pepper and remaining ingredients until a smooth paste is formed. Set aside.

continued on next page

BOUILLABAISSE (CONTINUED)

Seafood:

¼	pound large shrimp
2	1½-2 pound lobsters, cut up, shells cracked
½	pound red snapper filet, cut into bite-sized pieces
1	pound mussels
1	pound large sea scallops
10	1-inch slices toasted French bread

Peel and devein the shrimp, leaving the tails intact. Bring the bouillon to a boil. Add the lobster. Boil for 5 minutes longer. Add the snapper. Boil for another 5 minutes. Add the shrimp, mussels and scallops. Continue boiling, partially covered, for approximately 10 minutes longer or until the shrimp turn pink and the mussels open. Discard any mussels that do not.

To serve, ladle the fish and broth into a large, wide-mouthed soup tureen. Thin the rouille with 2 teaspoons of broth and place in a gravy boat or small bowl. Place a bread slice into each soup bowl and ladle the fish and broth over top. Spoon a dollop of the rouille on top of each bowl and have your guests mix it together.

The rouille is a very important addition to the Bouillabaisse because it enhances the flavor of the broth as well as the seafood. Be patient when attempting this recipe for the first time — with a little practice, you'll be ready to impress your friends.

FRANCE

LIGHT FRENCH ONION SOUP

(Serves 6)

Prep Time: 20 minutes
Cook Time: 50-55 minutes

Nutritional Analysis
per serving

Calories	*258*
Fat	*9 g*
Sodium	*839 mg*
Protein	*12 g*
Carbohydrates	*31 g*
Cholesterol	*16 mg*

Soup:

6	cups thinly sliced onion
2	tablespoons olive oil
3	tablespoons all-purpose flour
2	quarts defatted chicken or turkey stock
½	teaspoon salt

In a large pot, sauté the onion in 2 tablespoons of the olive oil until golden. Add the flour. Cook for 2 minutes, stirring occasionally. Remove from heat. In a separate saucepan, heat the stock until hot, but not boiling. Stir into the onion mixture. Simmer the soup, partially covered, for 35 minutes. Add the salt.

Topping:

6	1-inch thick slices French bread
1	teaspoon olive oil
2	garlic cloves, minced
1½	cups grated nonfat Swiss or Parmesan cheese

Preheat oven to 350°. Place the bread slices on a baking sheet. Bake for approximately 10 to 12 minutes or until crispy. Mix the olive oil and minced garlic. Brush the mixture on top of the toasted bread. To serve, place the bread slices into 6 individual soup bowls and ladle the hot soup over top. Sprinkle with equal amounts of the grated cheese. Serve very hot.

To vary the cheese topping, place a slice of nonfat Swiss cheese on top of each bowl of soup and broil until slightly brown and bubbly. Be sure to use oven-proof bowls.

VEGETABLE SOUP WITH BASIL

(Serves 12)

Soup:

3	cups water
1	cup dried white beans
1	tablespoon minced garlic
1½	cups finely chopped onion
2	tablespoons olive oil
2	cups coarsely chopped, seeded, peeled tomatoes
2	quarts water
1	cup dry white wine
1¼	cups each dried carrots and diced potatoes
1	cup coarsely chopped leeks
¾	cup coarsely chopped celery
1¼	cups each diced zucchini and sliced green beans
1	cup coarsely chopped fresh basil
2	teaspoons salt
2	teaspoons black pepper
	pistou (see below)

Prep Time: 35 minutes
Cook Time: 2 hours

Nutritional Analysis
per serving

Calories	*171*
Fat	*4 g*
Sodium	*393 mg*
Protein	*5 g*
Carbohydrates	*26 g*
Cholesterol	*less than 1 mg*

In a 3-quart pot, bring the water to a boil. Add the beans. Simmer, partially covered, for 1 hour or until tender. Drain, reserving the liquid. Set both aside. In a large pot, sauté the garlic and onion in the olive oil until golden. Add the tomato. Cook over medium heat for 3 minutes. Add the 2 quarts of water. Bring to a boil over high heat. Add the wine, all vegetables, basil, cooked beans and reserved liquid. Reduce heat and simmer, uncovered, for 20 minutes or until tender. Add the salt and pepper.

Pistou (thick paste to enhance flavor):

4	garlic cloves, minced
¾	cup coarsely chopped fresh basil
3	tablespoons tomato paste
1	tablespoon olive oil
½	cup finely crumbled day-old French bread

In a food processor, blend all ingredients until smooth. To serve, ladle the soup into a tureen and stir in the pistou until well blended.

FRANCE

Prep Time: 30 minutes
Cook Time: 50 minutes
Misc Time: Chill 4 hours
*   to overnight*

Nutritional Analysis
per serving

Calories	*145*
Fat	*3 g*
Sodium	*421 mg*
Protein	*4 g*
Carbohydrates	*25 g*
Cholesterol	*10 mg*

VICHYSSOISE (LEEK AND POTATO SOUP)

(Serves 8)

5	cups coarsely chopped, peeled potatoes
4	cups thinly sliced leeks (use most of the white part with a small amount of green for color)
2½	quarts defatted chicken stock or water
1	teaspoon salt
2	teaspoons ground white pepper
⅓	cup lowfat milk
¼	cup finely chopped parsley

In a large saucepan, bring the potatoes, leeks, chicken stock or water and salt to a boil. Simmer, partially covered, for approximately 45 minutes or until tender. Ladle into a food processor a small amount at a time and blend until semi-smooth. After processing, empty into a large bowl and set aside. Once all of the soup has a semi-smooth consistency, return it to the saucepan. Sprinkle with the white pepper. Mix in the milk. Cool. Chill, covered, for 4 hours to overnight. To serve, ladle into individual bowls and sprinkle with the parsley.

Vichyssoise is one of the best known French soups. It's refreshing for lunch on a hot summer afternoon or as an appetizer on a warm evening.

CHICKEN WITH SWEET PEPPERS

(Serves 8)

8	4-ounce boneless, skinless chicken breasts, pounded thin
1	cup all-purpose flour
3	tablespoons olive oil
½	cup finely chopped shallots
1	cup thinly sliced red bell pepper
1	cup defatted chicken stock
1	cup dry white wine
¼	cup finely chopped parsley
	parsley sprigs for garnish

Prep Time: 25 minutes
Cook Time: 20 minutes

Nutritional Analysis
per serving

Calories	*271*
Fat	*8 g*
Sodium	*80 mg*
Protein	*30 g*
Carbohydrates	*13 g*
Cholesterol	*74 mg*

In a bowl, dredge the chicken breasts in flour on both sides. In a large skillet, heat 2 tablespoons of the olive oil. Add the chicken. Cook for approximately 6 to 8 minutes or until well browned. Remove the chicken to a heated platter and set aside. Add the remaining 1 tablespoon of olive oil to the skillet. Add the shallots and red pepper. Sauté until slightly browned. Return the chicken to the skillet. Add the chicken stock, wine and parsley. Cook, uncovered, over medium heat for approximately 3 minutes or until the liquid has been reduced by ⅓ and the chicken is tender. To serve, place the chicken into a large dish and spoon the sauce over top. Garnish with parsley sprigs.

FRANCE

Coq Au Vin (Chicken in Wine Sauce)

(Serves 8)

Prep Time: 25 minutes
Cook Time: 35-40 minutes

Nutritional Analysis
per serving

Calories	*234*
Fat	*6 g*
Sodium	*83 mg*
Protein	*29 g*
Carbohydrates	*4 g*
Cholesterol	*74 mg*

8	large boneless, skinless chicken breasts, cut into halves
2	tablespoons olive oil
2	cups thickly sliced fresh mushrooms
1	teaspoon crushed dried thyme
2	teaspoons minced garlic
2	bay leaves
$\frac{1}{2}$	cup coarsely chopped parsley
$\frac{1}{4}$	cup finely chopped shallots
1	cup defatted chicken stock
2	cups dry wine (red or white)
	parsley sprigs for garnish

In a large skillet, sauté the chicken in the olive oil for approximately 6 to 8 minutes or until well browned. Add the mushrooms, thyme, garlic, bay leaves, parsley and shallots. Cook for 2 minutes over medium heat, stirring constantly. Add the chicken stock and wine. Simmer, uncovered, for approximately 30 minutes or until the chicken is tender and the liquid has been reduced by $\frac{1}{3}$. Discard the bay leaves. To serve, place the chicken into a large dish. Garnish with parsley sprigs.

COQUILLES PROVENÇALE

(Serves 8)

3	pounds large sea scallops
1	tablespoon minced garlic
2	tablespoons olive oil
½	teaspoon crushed red pepper
1	cup coarsely chopped, seeded, peeled tomatoes
½	cup dry white wine
1	tablespoon lemon juice
	chopped parsley for garnish

Drain the scallops and dry on paper towels. In a skillet, sauté the garlic in the olive oil until golden. Add the scallops and red pepper. Cook, stirring constantly, over high heat for approximately 2 minutes or until the scallops begin are slightly browned. Add the tomato, wine and lemon juice. Cook, stirring frequently, over medium heat for 2 minutes longer. Garnish with chopped parsley. Serve hot.

Prep Time: 20 minutes
Cook Time: 10 minutes

Nutritional Analysis
per serving

Calories	*331*
Fat	*5 g*
Sodium	*628 mg*
Protein	*63 g*
Carbohydrates	*7 g*
Cholesterol	*120 mg*

FRANCE

SALMON WITH GARLIC AND HERBS
(Serves 8)

Prep Time: 45 minutes
Cook Time: 15 minutes

Nutritional Analysis
per serving

Calories	*235*
Fat	*10 g*
Sodium	*335 mg*
Protein	*33 g*
Carbohydrates	*2 g*
Cholesterol	*56 mg*

1	tablespoon olive oil
¼	cup lemon juice
4	garlic cloves, minced
2	tablespoons crushed tarragon
2	tablespoons minced shallots
2	tablespoons finely chopped parsley
1	teaspoon salt
1	teaspoon black pepper
8	4-ounce salmon steaks
	lemon wedges for garnish

In a small bowl, combine the olive oil, lemon juice, garlic, tarragon, shallots, parsley, salt and pepper. Set aside. Place the salmon steaks on a rack in the oven broiler pan. Brush the herb mixture on both sides, reserving some for later use. Broil 8 inches from the heat source, carefully watching the fish as it cooks. Turn frequently to prevent burning. Baste often with the herb mixture to keep the salmon moist. Garnish with lemon wedges. Serve immediately.

SOLE WITH MUSHROOM-SHALLOT SAUCE
(Serves 8)

Sole:

	non-stick cooking spray
8	6-ounce sole filets (gray, lemon, etc.)

Preheat oven to 350°. Lightly coat a baking dish with the cooking spray. Fold the sole pieces in half and place in the baking dish. If the pieces are at least ¼ inch thick, there is no need to fold them in half.

Sauce

1	pound sliced fresh mushrooms
2	tablespoons finely chopped shallots
1	tablespoon finely chopped parsley
2	tablespoons olive oil
⅓	cup water
⅔	cup dry white wine
	lemon slices for garnish
	parsley sprigs for garnish

In a skillet, sauté the mushrooms, shallots and parsley in the olive oil until the mushrooms are browned. Place on top of the fish. Pour the water and wine into the baking dish. Bake, uncovered, for approximately 15 minutes or until the fish is tender and flaky, basting often. Garnish with lemon slices and parsley sprigs.

Prep Time: 25 minutes
Cook Time: 20 minutes

Nutritional Analysis per serving

Calories	258
Fat	5 g
Sodium	179 mg
Protein	45 g
Carbohydrates	3 g
Cholesterol	116 mg

FRANCE

CHEESE SOUFFLÉ
(Serves 8)

Prep Time: 25 minutes
Cook Time: 25-30 minutes

Nutritional Analysis
per serving

Calories	114
Fat	4 g
Sodium	467 mg
Protein	11 g
Carbohydrates	8 g
Cholesterol	4 mg

	non-stick cooking spray
⅓	cup grated nonfat Parmesan cheese
2	tablespoons olive oil
3	tablespoons all-purpose flour
1½	cups lowfat milk
½	teaspoon salt
¼	teaspoon white pepper
1	cup egg product
7	egg whites
1	cup grated nonfat Swiss cheese

Preheat oven to 375°. Coat a 2-quart soufflé dish with the cooking spray. Sprinkle with 1 tablespoon of the Parmesan cheese and set aside. In a saucepan, make a roux by heating the olive oil and stirring in the flour with a wire whisk. Cook over low heat for 1 minute, stirring constantly. Do not let the roux brown. Remove from heat. In another saucepan, warm the milk until hot, but not boiling. Add to the roux, beating rapidly until well blended. Add the salt and pepper. Cook over low heat, whisking constantly, for approximately 5 minutes or until the sauce bubbles and is smooth and thick. Remove from heat. Whisk in the egg product. Set aside. In a bowl, beat the egg whites with an electric mixer or wire whisk until stiff peaks form. Stir a large spoonful of the beaten egg whites into the sauce. Reserve 2 tablespoons of the remaining Parmesan cheese and set aside. Stir the remaining Parmesan cheese and Swiss cheese into the sauce. Carefully fold in the remaining beaten egg whites until well blended. Pour into the prepared dish. Sprinkle with the reserved Parmesan cheese.

Cut a trench around the dish 1½ inches deep and 1 inch from the rim with a knife or spatula. The center will form a "cap" when baked. Place the soufflé on the middle oven rack and reduce the heat to 350°. Bake, uncovered, for approximately 25 to 30 minutes or until the soufflé puffs above the rim of the dish and the top is slightly browned. Serve immediately.

MUSHROOM AND LEEK QUICHE

(Serves 8)

Pastry:

	non-stick cooking spray
2	cups all-purpose flour
2	tablespoons solid vegetable shortening
	ice water
½	teaspoon salt

Prep Time: 40 minutes
Cook Time: 25-30 minutes

Nutritional Analysis
per serving

Calories	*188*
Fat	*4 g*
Sodium	*636 mg*
Protein	*9 g*
Carbohydrates	*29 g*
Cholesterol	*5 mg*

Preheat oven to 325°. Lightly coat a 9-inch round baking dish with the cooking spray. In a bowl, mix the flour and shortening with a fork or pastry cutter until coarse. Add enough water and salt to form a soft dough. Roll into a ball with floured hands and place on a floured surface. Roll out into a circle large enough to fit generously into the prepared baking dish. Flute the edge decoratively. Set aside while making the filling.

Filling:

3	cups lowfat milk
⅓	cup egg product
1	cup thinly sliced fresh mushrooms
1	cup finely chopped leeks
1	teaspoon salt
1	cup grated fat-free Swiss or Mozzarella cheese

In a bowl, beat the milk and egg product with a wire whisk until blended. Stir in the remaining ingredients. Mix well.

To assemble, pour the filling into the pastry shell. Bake on the center oven rack for approximately 25 to 30 minutes or until the filling is set and the top is slightly browned.

This quiche may be served in smaller appetizer portions or in larger luncheon portions accompanied by fresh fruit.

FRANCE

BAKED TOMATOES PROVENÇALE
(Serves 8)

Prep Time: 20 minutes
Cook Time: 20-25 minutes

Nutritional Analysis
per serving

Calories	*122*
Fat	*3 g*
Sodium	*420 mg*
Protein	*4 g*
Carbohydrates	*20 g*
Cholesterol	*1 mg*

Tomatoes:

8	large, firm, ripe tomatoes

Preheat oven to 350°. Cut the tomatoes into halves crosswise. Scoop out the seeds with a small spoon. Drain upside-down on paper towels while preparing the filling.

Filling:

	non-stick cooking spray
1½	cups dry coarse white bread crumbs
¾	cup finely chopped parsley
2	garlic cloves, minced
1	tablespoon olive oil
1	teaspoon salt
1	teaspoon black pepper
	fresh chopped parsley for garnish

Lightly coat a baking dish with the cooking spray. In a bowl, mix the bread crumbs, parsley, garlic, olive oil, salt and pepper.

To assemble, stuff the tomatoes evenly with the bread crumb mixture. Place them stuffed-side up into the prepared baking dish. Bake, uncovered, for approximately 20 to 25 minutes or until tender. If the bread crumb mixture begins to dry out while the tomatoes are baking, drizzle 1 teaspoon of water over each. Garnish with chopped parsley. Serve hot.

BASIL POTATOES

(Serves 8)

4	cups thinly sliced, peeled potatoes
2	teaspoons minced garlic
2	teaspoons minced shallots
2	tablespoons olive oil
2	tablespoons all-purpose flour
2	cups skim milk
1	cup minced fresh basil
	or 3 tablespoons dried basil
	fresh basil for garnish

In a large saucepan, bring water to a boil. Add the potatoes. Cook, partially covered, for approximately 20 minutes or until tender. Drain and set aside. In a large, deep pan, sauté the garlic and shallots in the olive oil until golden. Add the flour. Cook over medium heat, stirring constantly, until a roux is formed. Add the milk. Continue to stir constantly until the sauce thickens. Mix in the potatoes and minced basil. Cook for 5 minutes longer. To serve, pour the potatoes and sauce into a bowl. Garnish with fresh basil.

Prep Time: 45 minutes
Cook Time: 45 minutes

Nutritional Analysis
per serving

Calories	*133*
Fat	*3 g*
Sodium	*36 mg*
Protein	*4 g*
Carbohydrates	*20 g*
Cholesterol	*1 mg*

PARSLEY CARROTS

(Serves 8)

16	large carrots, peeled, sliced diagonally
1	teaspoon olive oil
2	tablespoons finely chopped fresh parsley

In a pot, steam the carrots for approximately 15 minutes or until tender, but still slightly crisp. Drain. To serve, place in a bowl and drizzle with the olive oil. Sprinkle with parsley. Serve immediately.

Prep Time: 15 minutes
Cook Time: 15-20 minutes

Nutritional Analysis
per serving

Calories	*67*
Fat	*1 g*
Sodium	*50 mg*
Protein	*1 g*
Carbohydrates	*21 g*
Cholesterol	*0 mg*

FRANCE

RATATOUILLE
(Serves 8)

Prep Time: 45 minutes
Cook Time: 25-30 minutes

Nutritional Analysis
per serving

Calories	*154*
Fat	*4 g*
Sodium	*32 mg*
Protein	*2 g*
Carbohydrates	*25 g*
Cholesterol	*0 mg*

2	pounds eggplant, peeled, sliced ³/₄-inch thick
3	pounds tomatoes, quartered, seeded
1	tablespoon minced garlic
3	cups thinly sliced onion
2	tablespoons olive oil
2	pounds zucchini, sliced ½-inch thick
2	cups julienned, seeded green bell pepper
½	cup dry white wine
½	cup finely chopped parsley

Drain the eggplant on paper towels for 10 minutes. Coarsely chop the tomatoes. In a large, wide pot, sauté the garlic and onion in the olive oil until golden. Add the eggplant, zucchini and green pepper. Sauté for approximately 2 minutes or until slightly browned. Add the tomato, wine and parsley. Simmer, partially covered, for approximately 20 minutes or until tender, stirring occasionally. Serve warm or cold.

FRANCE

RICE WITH SUN-DRIED TOMATOES

(Serves 6)

4	cups water
2	cups converted white rice
1	cup finely chopped onion
1	cup finely chopped green bell pepper
½	cup thinly sliced sun-dried tomatoes
1	teaspoon olive oil
½	teaspoon salt
1	teaspoon black pepper

In a pot, bring the water to a boil. Add the rice. Reduce heat and simmer, partially covered, for approximately 20 minutes or until tender and the water has been absorbed. In a skillet, sauté the onion, green pepper and tomato in the olive oil until slightly soft. To serve, combine the rice and vegetables in a large bowl. Toss well. Season with the salt and pepper.

Prep Time: 15 minutes
Cook Time: 20-25 minutes

Nutritional Analysis
per serving

Calories	*201*
Fat	*1 g*
Sodium	*191 mg*
Protein	*4 g*
Carbohydrates	*43 g*
Cholesterol	*0 mg*

FRANCE

CHOCOLATE MOUSSE

(Serves 4)

Prep Time: 25 minutes
Cook Time: 5 minutes
Misc Time: Chill 6 hours
            to overnight

Nutritional Analysis
per serving

Calories   150
Fat   1 g
Sodium   87 mg
Protein   7 g
Carbohydrates   28 g
Cholesterol   less than 1 mg

6	tablespoons cocoa powder
8	tablespoons sugar
5	tablespoons skim milk
2	tablespoons egg product
4	egg whites
¼	teaspoon cream of tartar

In a small saucepan, combine the cocoa powder and sugar. Mix thoroughly. Gradually add the milk, stirring constantly, over medium heat. Cook, beating constantly with a wire whisk, for approximately 5 minutes or until thoroughly blended and the sugar has dissolved. Stir in the egg product. Remove from heat. Pour the cocoa mixture into a medium bowl. Cool for 15 minutes. In another bowl, beat the egg whites and cream of tartar until stiff peaks form. Gradually fold into the cocoa mixture. Spoon the mousse into individual serving dishes. Chill, uncovered, for 6 hours to overnight before serving.

GRAND MARNIER CRÊPES

(Makes 12/Serves 6)

Prep Time: 35 minutes
Cook Time: 40 minutes
Misc Time: Chill 1 hour

Nutritional Analysis
per serving

Calories   298
Fat   1 g
Sodium   58 mg
Protein   8 g
Carbohydrates   43 g
Cholesterol   3 mg

Crêpes:

2	cups all-purpose flour
½	cup egg product
1½	cups lowfat milk
2	tablespoons sugar
	non-stick cooking spray

In a food processor, combine the flour, egg product, milk and sugar. Blend for 5 seconds. Scrape the side of the bowl and blend for 30 seconds longer. Chill the batter, covered, for at least 1 hour before cooking. Coat a crêpe pan or small skillet with the cooking spray and warm over high heat. Ladle 3 tablespoons of the batter into the pan

continued on next page

GRAND MARNIER CRÊPES (CONTINUED)

and tip the pan until the batter covers the bottom. Pour off any excess as the crêpe should be very thin. Cook for approximately 1 minute on each side or until the edges turn brown. Slide onto a plate. Repeat the process with the remaining batter. If the batter begins to thicken, add drops of water to thin it out. The crêpes may be stacked on top of each other and covered with plastic wrap to keep them from drying out.

Filling:

16	ounces nonfat cream cheese, softened
¼	cup confectioners' sugar
2	teaspoons grated orange peel

In a bowl, beat the cream cheese, confectioners' sugar and orange peel until smooth.

To assemble, place 2 tablespoons of the filling in the center of each crêpe. Fold in half and then in half again. When all crêpes have been filled, set them aside.

Sauce:

1	cup Grand Marnier liqueur
½	cup freshly squeezed orange juice

In a shallow pan, warm the liqueur and orange juice over high heat until the mixture is very hot. Place the crêpes into the pan. Heat for approximately 5 minutes or until hot, covering each completely with the sauce. Serve immediately.

FRANCE

STRAWBERRY TARTS

(Makes 6/Serves 6)

Prep Time: 40 minutes
Cook Time: 25 minutes
Misc Time: Chill 3½-4½ hours

Nutritional Analysis
per serving

Calories	406
Fat	7 g
Sodium	84 mg
Protein	12 g
Carbohydrates	72 g
Cholesterol	3 mg

Pastry:

2	cups all-purpose flour
3	tablespoons solid vegetable shortening
	ice water

Preheat oven to 375°. In a bowl, blend the flour and shortening with a fork or pastry cutter until coarse. Gradually add enough water to form a soft dough. Place on a floured surface and roll out to ¼-inch thickness. Cut out in round pieces to fit six 4-inch individual tart shells. Place the pastry into the shells and flute the edges. Pierce the bottoms of the shells with the tines of a fork. Place on a baking sheet. Bake, uncovered, for approximately 15 to 20 minutes or until golden.

Custard:

1½	cups lowfat milk
½	cup egg product
⅓	cup sugar
¼	cup all-purpose flour
1	envelope unflavored gelatin
1	tablespoon hot water
1	teaspoon vanilla extract
3	egg whites

In a small saucepan, warm the milk. Set aside. In a larger saucepan, beat the egg product and sugar for 2 minutes with a wire whisk. Add the flour, whisking constantly. In a cup, soften the gelatin with the hot water. Mix the softened gelatin and vanilla into the contents of the larger saucepan. Slowly add the warm milk, whisking constantly. Cook, whisking constantly, over medium heat for approximately 8 minutes or until the custard is smooth and thickened. Do not allow it to boil. Pour the custard into a bowl. Chill, uncovered, for 20 minutes. In another bowl, beat the egg whites until stiff peaks form. Fold the egg whites into the chilled custard.

continued on next page

STRAWBERRY TARTS (CONTINUED)

Strawberries and Glaze:

1	cup low-calorie strawberry jelly
1	tablespoon hot water
1	tablespoon Kirsch liqueur
1½	quarts ripe strawberries, stems removed

In a small saucepan, warm the jelly and hot water over low heat until thickened, stirring constantly. Remove from heat. Stir in the liqueur. Cool slightly.

To assemble, spoon the custard into the prepared tart shells. Arrange the strawberries, stem-side down, on top of the shells until each tart is completely covered. Spoon the warm glaze over the berries. Chill, uncovered, for 3 to 4 hours before serving.

For a change of pace, other berries may be substituted — raspberries, blueberries and blackberries make delicious tarts as well. Don't forget to use the same flavor of jelly as the fruit.

FRANCE

RASPBERRY SOUFFLÉ

(Serves 4)

Prep Time: 40 minutes
Cook Time: 25-30 minutes
Misc Time: Chill 20 minutes

Nutritional Analysis
per serving

Calories	194
Fat	less than 1 g
Sodium	195 mg
Protein	13 g
Carbohydrates	30 g
Cholesterol	0 mg

	non-stick cooking spray
1	cup egg product
⅓	cup sugar
2	cups strained, puréed raspberries
2	tablespoons raspberry liqueur
8	egg whites
¼	teaspoon cream of tartar
2	tablespoons confectioners' sugar

Preheat oven to 375°. Coat a 1½-quart soufflé dish with the cooking spray. In a pot, cook the egg product, sugar and raspberries over medium heat for 2 minutes, stirring constantly. Remove from heat. Cool. Stir in the liqueur. Chill, uncovered, for 20 minutes. In a large bowl, beat the egg whites and cream of tartar at high speed using an electric mixer or by hand with a wire whisk until stiff peaks form. Stir a large spoonful of the beaten egg whites into the raspberry mixture. Using a rubber spatula, gently fold in the remaining egg whites. Spoon into the prepared dish, filling 2 inches below the top. Smooth with the spatula. Cut a trench around the dish 1½ inches deep and 1 inch from the rim with the spatula. The center will form a "cap" when baked. Bake, uncovered, on the middle oven rack for 3 minutes. Reduce temperature to 350°. Bake for approximately 25 to 30 minutes longer or until the soufflé puffs above the rim of the dish and the top is slightly browned. Sprinkle with the confectioners' sugar. Serve immediately.

For an extra special touch, drizzle a tablespoonful of raspberry liqueur over each serving.

Facing page — Greece (pictured clockwise): Chicken with Okra, Almond Cake, Stuffed Mussels, Stuffed Grape Leaves, Moussaka

GREECE

Beverage Suggestions

WINE

Appetizers	• Retsina (dry white)
Poultry	• Ropa (traditional red)
Seafood	• Robola (dry white) • Verdeal (dry white)
Vegetables	• Kokkineli (rosé)
Desserts	• Pale Golden Muscat of Samos

BEER

Bean Soup	• Bock • Porter
Turkey/Quail	• Mild Ale • Amber Lager
Chicken/Seafood	• Pilsner • Weisse
Vegetables/Vegetable Soup	• Pilsner
Fruit Desserts	• Lambic • Weisse

COFFEE

Benizelos Filter Coffee
Loumidas Filter Coffee
Espresso Roast

GREECE

$\mathcal{A}$ few years ago my family and I took a wonderful vacation to Greece. My plan was to visit the historical sights I had studied about in school and to learn all I could about one of my all-time favorite cuisines.

Athens was our first stop. It looked just like the ancient city I remembered from my textbooks. The streets were lined with quaint restaurants that specialized in seafood, eggplant and chicken dishes. One area in particular, the Plaka, was a unique and impressive mecca of shopping and dining. The restaurant owners and chefs (many times the very same person) were very friendly and more than willing to allow me into their kitchens to receive instruction. I marveled at the simplicity with which the foods were prepared. Many even subscribed to my own personal philosophy on healthy cooking — using only the freshest ingredients available and olive oil in sparing amounts.

Much of what I learned there was the more popular, stereotypical Greek cuisine — Chicken with Okra, Swordfish, Souvlaki, and Spinach Pie — a dish many Americans are familiar with. The classic Greek version made with feta cheese, Spanakotiropita, is often mistaken for Spanakopita, the version made *without* cheese. This is a classic example of something lost in translation. Quite often the latter is featured in restaurants, which is somewhat confusing because you expect it to contain cheese. I personally prefer the Greek version without cheese because it's a thinner pie, allowing instead for the taste of the spinach and seasonings to prevail.

Additionally, I tasted Eggplant Grecia for the first time. What a flavor! The unpeeled eggplant combined with garlic, onion and tomato was a must-learn for my book. And who could study Greek cooking without learning the inside secrets of Baklava? Although the native preparation uses a generous amount of butter, I vowed to make a lowfat version without sacrificing the flavor we Baklava-lovers are accustomed to.

The recipes featured in this section are representative of some of the most popular dishes from Greece. Enjoy the true flavors of the vegetables, chicken and seafood just as the Greek people do, in a light and delicious manner.

GREECE

MARINATED FRUIT SALAD

(Serves 12)

Prep Time: 35 minutes
Misc Time: Marinate 1 hour

Nutritional Analysis
per serving

Calories	102
Fat	0 g
Sodium	2 mg
Protein	1 g
Carbohydrates	21 g
Cholesterol	0 mg

2	large oranges, peeled, seeded
2	ripe pears, peeled
2	ripe bananas, peeled
2	cups seedless red grapes
2	cups seedless green grapes
1	teaspoon sugar
½	cup lemon juice
1	cup dry white wine

Cut the oranges, pears and bananas into bite-sized pieces. In a serving bowl, combine all fruit and the sugar. Pour the lemon juice and wine over top. Toss lightly. Chill, covered, for at least 1 hour. Gently toss again before serving.

It's hard to believe that something this delicious has absolutely no fat and no cholesterol. And besides, the colors of the fruit make this dish a most beautiful centerpiece.

GREECE

CABBAGE SALAD

(Serves 8)

1	medium head red cabbage
1	medium head green cabbage
2	cups grated carrots
½	cup finely chopped onion
2	tablespoons olive oil
½	cup wine vinegar
¾	cup fat-free mayonnaise
2	tablespoons water

Shred the cabbage with a knife into long, loose threads. In a salad bowl, combine the cabbage, carrots, onion, olive oil, wine vinegar, mayonnaise and water. Mix thoroughly.

It doesn't have to take a lot of time to make fun, creative salads. Cabbage salad is an easy and colorful addition to your international meal.

Prep Time: 25 minutes

*Nutritional Analysis
per serving*

Calories	*124*
Fat	*4 g*
Sodium	*267 mg*
Protein	*2 g*
Carbohydrates	*21 g*
Cholesterol	*0 mg*

GREECE

POTATO SALAD
(Serves 6)

Prep Time: 35 minutes
Cook Time: 20 minutes

Nutritional Analysis
per serving

Calories	148
Fat	4 g
Sodium	308 mg
Protein	1 g
Carbohydrates	25 g
Cholesterol	0 mg

1	pound potatoes (red or white)
½	cup freshly squeezed lemon juice
1	cup thinly sliced onion
1	cup coarsely chopped parsley
2	tablespoons olive oil
¾	cup fat-free mayonnaise
¼	teaspoon black pepper
2	tablespoons water

Wash the potatoes thoroughly. In a pot, bring water to a boil. Add the potatoes with the skins still on. Cook, partially covered, for approximately 20 minutes or until tender. Drain. Peel before completely cooled. Cut into circular slices and place into a bowl. Pour in the lemon juice. Add the onion and parsley. Mix in the olive oil, mayonnaise, pepper and water. Blend thoroughly.

Here's a healthy variation of Greek potato salad without all the fat.

LENTIL SOUP

(Serves 6)

1	pound lentil beans
1	medium onion, finely chopped
10	garlic cloves, minced
6	bay leaves
2	cups crushed, peeled tomatoes
4	cups water
½	cup red wine vinegar
¼	cup olive oil
½	teaspoon black pepper

In a stockpot, add enough water to cover the beans. Bring the water to a boil. Cook, partially covered, for 10 minutes. Drain and discard the water. Return the beans to the stockpot. Add the onion, garlic, bay leaves, tomato and water. Simmer, partially covered, for approximately 35 to 40 minutes or until the beans are tender. Add more water as needed to provide the desired thickness. Stir in the vinegar, olive oil and pepper. Discard the bay leaves before serving.

Prep Time: 25 minutes
Cook Time: 45 minutes

Nutritional Analysis
per serving

Calories	*329*
Fat	*9 g*
Sodium	*196 mg*
Protein	*15 g*
Carbohydrates	*46 g*
Cholesterol	*0 mg*

GREECE

VEGETABLE SOUP GRECIA

(Serves 6)

Prep Time: 25 minutes
Cook Time: 20 minutes

Nutritional Analysis
per serving

Calories	*195*
Fat	*7 g*
Sodium	*227 mg*
Protein	*2 g*
Carbohydrates	*31 g*
Cholesterol	*0 mg*

4	medium potatoes, peeled, diced
1	medium onion, thinly sliced
4	medium carrots, peeled, diced
½	cup coarsely chopped celery
1	cup sliced squash
1	cup sliced zucchini
2	cups crushed, peeled tomatoes
2	teaspoons crushed oregano
3	bay leaves
3	tablespoons olive oil

In a large stockpot, combine the potatoes, onion, carrots, celery, squash, zucchini, tomato, oregano and bay leaves. Cover with water. Bring to a rapid boil. Continue to boil for 5 minutes longer. Reduce heat and simmer, partially covered, for approximately 15 minutes or until the vegetables are tender. Add the oil. Discard the bay leaves before serving.

GREECE

LEMON CHICKEN

(Serves 8)

Chicken:
| 8 | large chicken breasts, skinned |

Place the chicken breasts in a large baking pan. Set aside.

Marinade:
3	medium lemons, freshly squeezed
½	cup white wine
2	tablespoons olive oil
3	garlic cloves, minced
½	cup finely chopped parsley
	parsley sprigs for garnish
	lemon slices for garnish

In a bowl, mix the lemon juice, wine, olive oil, garlic and parsley. Pour over the chicken. Marinate, covered, in the refrigerator for 4 hours.

Preheat oven to 350°. Bake the chicken for approximately 45 to 50 minutes or until tender, turning often to absorb the flavor of the marinade and to keep it moist. Remove the chicken to a heated platter. Garnish with parsley sprigs and thin lemon slices.

Serve this dish with an accompaniment of Oven-Roasted Potatoes (see page 66) for a delicious meal.

Prep Time: 25 minutes
Cook Time: 45-50 minutes
Misc Time: Marinate 4 hours

Nutritional Analysis
per serving

Calories	188
Fat	6 g
Sodium	66 mg
Protein	29 g
Carbohydrates	2 g
Cholesterol	73 mg

GREECE

CHICKEN WITH OKRA
(Serves 8)

Prep Time: 20 minutes
Cook Time: 60-65 minutes

Nutritional Analysis
per serving

Calories	*257*
Fat	*9 g*
Sodium	*209 mg*
Protein	*30 g*
Carbohydrates	*12 g*
Cholesterol	*73 mg*

2	large onions, thinly sliced
3	garlic cloves, minced
¼	cup olive oil
8	chicken breasts, skinned
1	pound fresh okra, stems removed
8	large, ripe tomatoes, peeled, crushed
½	cup finely chopped parsley
1	teaspoon crushed red pepper
¼	teaspoon black pepper
½	teaspoon salt

Preheat oven to 350°. In a skillet, sauté the onion and garlic in the olive oil until golden. Add the chicken. Cook, uncovered, over high heat for approximately 6 to 8 minutes or until well browned. Remove to a large baking dish. Add the okra, tomato, parsley, red pepper, black pepper and salt to the skillet. Reduce heat to medium and cook for approximately 10 minutes longer, stirring frequently. Pour over the chicken. Bake, covered, for approximately 40 minutes or until tender.

CHICKEN SHISH KABOBS

(Serves 8)

Kabobs:

8	boneless chicken breasts, cut into 1-inch square pieces
2	large onions, peeled, cut into 1-inch square pieces
2	large green bell peppers, seeded, cut into 1-inch square pieces

To arrange the skewers, begin with the chicken, then onion, then chicken again, then green pepper until all of the pieces have been used. Place the completed skewers into a shallow pan.

Marinade:

2	tablespoons olive oil
1	cup freshly squeezed lemon juice
2	tablespoons crushed oregano
½	cup red wine vinegar
6	garlic cloves, minced

In a bowl, combine the olive oil, lemon juice, oregano, wine vinegar and garlic. Pour over the skewers. Marinate, covered, in the refrigerator for 1 hour to overnight.

Preheat grill to a high flame. Drain the kabobs, reserving the marinade. Reduce the flame to medium and grill for approximately 25 minutes or until the chicken is tender and brown. Baste frequently with the reserved marinade to keep the kabobs moist.

I like to serve shish kabobs as the focal point of the table. Display them on a platter and let everyone take as much or as little as they want.

Prep Time: 30 minutes
Cook Time: 25 minutes
Misc Time: Marinate 1 hour
to overnight

Nutritional Analysis
per serving

Calories	*206*
Fat	*6 g*
Sodium	*65 mg*
Protein	*29 g*
Carbohydrates	*7 g*
Cholesterol	*73 mg*

Prep Time: 20 minutes
Cook Time: 25 minutes

Nutritional Analysis
per serving

Calories	*440*
Fat	*6 g*
Sodium	*241 mg*
Protein	*37 g*
Carbohydrates	*57 g*
Cholesterol	*73 mg*

SOUVLAKI OF CHICKEN IN PITA

(Serves 8)

Chicken:

8	boneless chicken breasts, skinned, cut into 1-inch square pieces

Preheat grill to a high flame. Divide the chicken pieces into 8 equal portions and place on skewers. Reduce the flame to medium and grill for approximately 15 minutes or until tender. Keep the chicken warm.

Sauce:

2	tablespoons olive oil
½	cup finely chopped parsley
2	tablespoons crushed oregano
1	teaspoon crushed red pepper

In a bowl, mix the olive oil, parsley, oregano and red pepper.

Pita:

8	pieces pita bread (plain or whole wheat)
2	large onions, thinly sliced
2	large firm tomatoes, thinly sliced

Lightly brush 1 side of each piece of pita bread with the sauce. Grill oiled-side down for 5 minutes or until slightly browned.

To assemble, place a skewer of chicken on the grilled side of each pita and fold around the chicken. Remove the skewer. Place the onion and tomato on top of the chicken. Roll the pita around its contents and wrap foil or wax paper halfway up each roll so that it stays together.

MOUSSAKA

(Serves 12)

Filling:

	non-stick cooking spray
4	large eggplant, peeled
1	teaspoon salt
1	pound ground turkey breast
3	medium onions, finely chopped
2	tablespoons olive oil
6	tomatoes, peeled, seeded, finely chopped
½	cup white wine

Prep Time: 45 minutes
Cook Time: 1½ hours

Nutritional Analysis
per serving

Calories	*220*
Fat	*5 g*
Sodium	*53 mg*
Protein	*15 g*
Carbohydrates	*27 g*
Cholesterol	*29 mg*

Preheat oven to 350°. Lightly coat a large baking dish with the cooking spray. Cut the eggplant into thin, round slices. Sprinkle with 1 teaspoon of salt and drain on paper towels. In a skillet, brown the turkey and onion in the olive oil. Add the tomato and wine. Cook over medium heat until ⅓ of the moisture has been absorbed. Place the eggplant slices on a baking sheet and cover with foil. Bake for approximately 25 to 30 minutes or until tender. Layer ½ of the eggplant slices, ground turkey mixture and remaining eggplant slices in the baking dish.

Mashed Potato Topping:

4	cups cubed, peeled white potatoes
1	cup skim milk
1	tablespoon olive oil

In a pot, bring water to a boil. Add the potatoes. Reduce heat to medium-high and cook, partially covered, for approximately 25 to 30 minutes or until tender. Drain. Return the potatoes to the pot. Add the milk and olive oil. Whip until creamy. Spread the topping evenly over the filling. Increase the oven temperature to 375°. Bake for 25 minutes or until the potatoes are browned and crispy on top.

This is an extremely light version of Moussaka, one of the most popular and well-known Greek dishes. Usually the eggplant is fried and the sauce contains beef or lamb. The mashed potatoes give the topping a creamy consistency without the fat of a heavy sauce.

GREECE

Prep Time: 30 minutes
Cook Time: 50 minutes

Nutritional Analysis
per serving

Calories	*59*
Fat	*2 g*
Sodium	*257 mg*
Protein	*4 g*
Carbohydrates	*5 g*
Cholesterol	*7 mg*

STUFFED GRAPE LEAVES

(Makes 36/Serves 18)

Grape Leaves:

36	grape vine leaves (in a jar)

Flatten and drain the grape leaves on paper towels.

Filling:

1	cup long grain white rice
1	cup ground turkey breast
1	teaspoon olive oil (to brown turkey)
2	tablespoons olive oil
1¼	cups finely chopped onion
½	cup finely chopped dill
2	teaspoons crushed mint
1	teaspoon black pepper
2	medium lemons, freshly squeezed

In a pot, bring water to a boil. Add the rice. Reduce heat and simmer, partially covered, for approximately 15 minutes or until the rice is still firm. Drain and set aside. In a skillet, sauté the turkey in 1 teaspoon of olive oil until well browned. In a bowl, mix the rice, turkey, 2 tablespoons of olive oil, onion, dill, mint and black pepper.

To assemble, spoon an equal amount of the filling onto each grape leaf and roll up to enclose the contents. Tuck the outer edges of the leaf under the bottom. Place the stuffed leaves into a large skillet or pan. Pour the lemon juice over top. Fill the pan halfway with water so that the grape leaves don't dry out during the cooking process. Place a weight such as a skillet lid on top of the leaves to prevent them from opening during cooking. Cook over medium heat for approximately 25 minutes or until the water has been absorbed and the rice is tender.

QUAIL WITH RICE

(Serves 8)

	non-stick olive oil cooking spray
16	whole quail
2	teaspoons minced garlic
¾	cup finely chopped parsley
½	cup lemon juice
2	tablespoons crushed oregano
½	cup dry white wine
1	teaspoon salt
2	teaspoons black pepper
2	cups long grain white rice
4	cups water
	lemon wedges for garnish

Prep Time: 25 minutes
Cook Time: 40 minutes

Nutritional Analysis
per serving

Calories	*358*
Fat	*12 g*
Sodium	*337 mg*
Protein	*24 g*
Carbohydrates	*34 g*
Cholesterol	*73 mg*

Coat a large skillet with the cooking spray and warm over high heat. Add the quail and garlic, searing the quail on both sides. Reduce heat to medium and cook for 5 minutes longer. Add the parsley, lemon juice, oregano, wine, salt, pepper, rice and water. Bring to a boil, stirring constantly. Reduce heat and simmer, partially covered, for 30 minutes or until the liquid has been absorbed. Remove to a heated serving platter. Garnish with lemon wedges.

GREECE

STUFFED MUSSELS

(Makes 24/Serves 8)

Prep Time: 30 minutes
Cook Time: 40-45 minutes

Nutritional Analysis
per serving

Calories	382
Fat	8 g
Sodium	553 mg
Protein	31 g
Carbohydrates	43 g
Cholesterol	64 mg

Mussels:

24	large mussels
3	cups water
½	cup white wine

Clean the mussels thoroughly. In a medium saucepan, combine the mussels, water and wine. Cover the pan and bring the liquid to a boil. Cook for approximately 10 minutes longer or until the mussels open. Remove from heat and allow the mussels to cool in the liquid. Discard any that did not open. Drain the mussels, reserving the cooking liquid. Set both aside.

Stuffing:

2	medium onions, finely chopped
4	garlic cloves, minced
2	tablespoons olive oil
2	cups converted white rice
2	tablespoons finely chopped parsley
1	teaspoon salt
1	teaspoon black pepper

In a skillet, sauté the onion and garlic in the olive oil until golden. Add the rice, parsley, salt and pepper. Cook over medium heat, stirring frequently, for approximately 5 minutes or until slightly browned.

To assemble, fill the mussels equally with the stuffing. Close the shells as tightly as possible and place into a shallow pan. Add the reserved cooking liquid. Cook, covered, over low heat for approximately 20 minutes or until the rice is tender.

These mussels may be served either warm or cold. If the rice appears to be drying out before it is thoroughly cooked, add just enough water to finish the cooking process.

MARINATED SWORDFISH STEAKS

(Serves 6)

Marinade:

2	teaspoons olive oil
1	tablespoon worcestershire sauce
¾	cup lemon juice
4	garlic cloves, minced
½	cup finely chopped onion
1	teaspoon crushed red pepper (optional)
1	tablespoon crushed oregano
2	tablespoons finely chopped parsley
1	teaspoon salt
1	teaspoon black pepper

In a large storage bowl with a lid, mix all ingredients. Set aside.

Swordfish:

6	4-ounce swordfish steaks
	parsley sprigs for garnish
	lemon wedges for garnish

Add the swordfish steaks to the marinade. Refrigerate, covered, for 4 hours to overnight. Preheat grill to a medium flame. Remove the swordfish steaks from the marinade. Grill for approximately 15 minutes or until fully cooked but not dry. Garnish with fresh parsley sprigs and lemon wedges.

Marinated Swordfish Steaks may also be cut into 1-inch cubes and placed alternately with wedges of green pepper, onion and tomatoes on small skewers and grilled as kabobs.

Prep Time: 25 minutes
Cook Time: 15-20 minutes
Misc Time: Marinate 4 hours
            to overnight

Nutritional Analysis
per serving

Calories	*172*
Fat	*6 g*
Sodium	*302 mg*
Protein	*24 g*
Carbohydrates	*4 g*
Cholesterol	*44 mg*

GREECE

Prep Time: 30 minutes
Cook Time: 35 minutes

Nutritional Analysis
per serving

Calories   107
Fat   4 g
Sodium   230 mg
Protein   5 g
Carbohydrates   8 g
Cholesterol   33 mg

GREEK STUFFED SHRIMP

(Serves 8)

Shrimp:

24   extra large shrimp

Preheat oven to 350°. Peel and devein the shrimp, leaving the tails intact. With a sharp knife, butterfly the shrimp by making a deep cut down the back from where the veins were removed. Set aside.

Stuffing:

5   garlic cloves, minced
1   cup finely chopped green onion
2   tablespoons olive oil
2   cups coarsely ground bread crumbs
1   tablespoon crushed oregano
½   cup lemon juice
1   teaspoon salt
1   teaspoon black pepper

1   cup dry white wine

In a large skillet, sauté the garlic and green onion in the olive oil until golden. Add the bread crumbs, oregano and lemon juice. Mix well. Season with the salt and pepper.

To assemble, arrange the shrimp, butterflied-side up, in a baking pan. Spoon an equal amount of stuffing onto each. Pour the wine into the baking pan. Bake, covered, for 25 minutes or until the shrimp turn pink, basting often with the wine. Do not overcook as the shrimp can become tough. Serve hot.

To vary this dish, substitute cooked white rice for the bread crumbs and follow the same procedure. Either version is equally delicious!

SQUID WITH RICE

(Serves 6)

1	pound squid
1	large onion, finely chopped
4	garlic cloves, minced
2	tablespoons olive oil
2	cups crushed, peeled tomatoes
1	teaspoon crushed fresh dill
	or 1 teaspoon dried dillweed
1	cup white wine
2	cups water
3	cups long grain white rice
	parsley sprigs for garnish

Prep Time: 25 minutes
Cook Time: 35-40 minutes

Nutritional Analysis
per serving

Calories	*442*
Fat	*5 g*
Sodium	*362 mg*
Protein	*12 g*
Carbohydrates	*81 g*
Cholesterol	*88 mg*

Remove and discard the tentacles of the squid. Make sure all of the cartilage has been removed. Cut into rings approximately ½ inch wide. Set aside in a bowl. In a skillet, sauté the onion and garlic in the olive oil until golden. Add the crushed tomato, dill and wine. Bring to a boil. Reduce heat to medium and cook, partially covered, for 10 minutes. Add the water and rice. Return to a boil. Reduce heat to medium and cook, partially covered, for approximately 10 minutes longer or until ½ of the liquid has been absorbed. Add the squid. Cook, partially covered, for approximately 5 minutes longer or until all of the liquid has been absorbed and the rice and squid are tender. Garnish with parsley sprigs. Serve immediately.

I personally think that the addition of a few tentacles gives more interest to this dish, especially from a presentation standpoint. The taste is the same without them, however.

GREECE

Prep Time: 25 minutes
Cook Time: 70 minutes

Nutritional Analysis
per serving

Calories	139
Fat	7 g
Sodium	155 mg
Protein	2 g
Carbohydrates	16 g
Cholesterol	0 mg

EGGPLANT GRECIA

(Serves 8)

4	eggplant
¼	cup olive oil
12	garlic cloves, minced
4	large onions, peeled, thinly sliced
8	large, ripe tomatoes, peeled, crushed
1	cup finely chopped parsley
1	teaspoon crushed red pepper
½	cup white wine

Preheat oven to 350°. Cut the eggplant into halves lengthwise and remove the stems. In a skillet, sauté the eggplant in ½ of the olive oil until browned. Remove to a baking dish. Add the garlic and onion to the skillet. Sauté until golden. Add the tomato, parsley, red pepper, white wine and remaining olive oil. Cook over medium heat for approximately 5 minutes. Pour the sauce over the eggplant. Bake, covered, for approximately 1 hour or until the eggplant is very soft.

So you've never tried eggplant before? This will be an amazing surprise. You'll be a fan forever!

STUFFED PEPPERS

(Serves 8)

Peppers:

8	large green bell peppers

Preheat oven to 350°. Cut the tops off the peppers, remove the seeds and set the tops aside. Place the peppers into a shallow baking dish.

Stuffing:

2	teaspoons minced garlic
½	cup finely chopped onion
	non-stick olive oil cooking spray
2	cups long grain white rice
1	cup coarsely chopped, seeded tomatoes
½	cup finely chopped parsley
½	teaspoon salt
5	cups water

Coat a large skillet with the cooking spray. Add the garlic and onion. Sauté until golden. Add the rice, tomato, parsley, salt and 4 cups of the water. Bring to a boil. Reduce heat and simmer, partially covered, for approximately 20 minutes or until the liquid has been absorbed and the rice is tender. Stir often.

To assemble, stuff the peppers with the rice mixture and place the tops back on. Pour 1 cup of water into the baking dish and cover loosely with foil. Bake for approximately 35 to 40 minutes or until tender.

Prep Time: 25 minutes
Cook Time: 1 hour

Nutritional Analysis
per serving

Calories	*166*
Fat	*0 g*
Sodium	*140 mg*
Protein	*3 g*
Carbohydrates	*38 g*
Cholesterol	*0 mg*

GREECE

OVEN-ROASTED POTATOES
(Serves 8)

Prep Time: 30 minutes
Cook Time: 35-40 minutes

Nutritional Analysis
per serving

Calories	138
Fat	less than 1 g
Sodium	145 mg
Protein	2 g
Carbohydrates	31 g
Cholesterol	0 mg

	non-stick olive oil cooking spray
2	pounds white potatoes, peeled
2	large onions, thinly sliced
2	tablespoons crushed oregano
½	cup finely chopped parsley
5	garlic cloves, minced
1	teaspoon salt
1	cup water

Preheat oven to 325°. Coat a baking dish with the cooking spray. Cut the potatoes into medium-sized pieces and place into the prepared dish. Mix in the onion, oregano, parsley, garlic and salt. Pour the water over the mixture and coat lightly with the cooking spray. Bake, covered, for approximately 25 to 30 minutes. Remove the cover and bake for 10 minutes longer or until the potatoes are tender. If they seem to be drying out during baking, sprinkle with additional water.

Serve Oven-Roasted Potatoes and Chicken with Okra (see page 54) for a wonderful combination.

SPINACH PIE (SPANAKOPITA)

(Serves 8)

Filling:

1	pound spinach (fresh or frozen)
⅔	cup egg product
½	cup finely chopped onion
1	teaspoon minced dill
1	teaspoon powdered nutmeg
1	teaspoon salt

Prep Time: 30 minutes
Cook Time: 40 minutes

Nutritional Analysis
per serving

Calories	89
Fat	0 g
Sodium	414 mg
Protein	4 g
Carbohydrates	16 g
Cholesterol	0 mg

Preheat oven to 350°. Wash the fresh spinach well and remove the stems. Or, thaw the frozen spinach and drain in a colander. Cut the spinach finely and rub vigorously with a paper towel to remove as much water as possible. In a bowl, combine the spinach, egg product, onion, dill, nutmeg and salt. Mix well.

Pastry:

	non-stick olive oil cooking spray
8	sheets ready-made phyllo pastry

Coat an 8-inch square baking dish lightly with the cooking spray. Line the dish with 4 sheets of phyllo pastry, coating lightly with the spray between layers. Spread the spinach mixture evenly over the pastry. Place the remaining 4 sheets of pastry on top of the spinach mixture, again coating lightly with the spray between layers. Trim the edge of the pastry around the baking dish. Bake, uncovered, for approximately 40 minutes or until golden brown. To serve, cut into 8 equal pieces. Serve slightly warm or at room temperature.

You'll never know you're eating the lowfat version of this Greek classic. It makes a tremendous difference when you use the non-stick olive oil spray instead of butter. Additionally, this version of Spinach Pie eliminates the feta cheese which makes it lighter and thinner.

ALMOND CAKE

(Serves 12)

Prep Time: 35 minutes
Cook Time: 55 minutes

Nutritional Analysis
per serving

Calories	275
Fat	8 g
Sodium	234 mg
Protein	7 g
Carbohydrates	41 g
Cholesterol	19 mg

Cake:

	non-stick cooking spray
	flour for dusting
1	cup sugar
1½	cups freshly ground bread crumbs
1½	cups all-purpose flour
1	tablespoon baking powder
1	teaspoon baking soda
2	tablespoons ground cinnamon
1	tablespoon ground cloves
1	cup lowfat milk
1	egg yolk
4	egg whites
2	cups sliced almonds

Preheat oven to 350°. Coat a tube pan with the cooking spray and dust with flour. In a large bowl, mix the sugar, bread crumbs, flour, baking powder, baking soda, cinnamon and cloves. In a smaller bowl, blend the milk, egg yolk and egg whites. Pour into the dry mixture, beating until all ingredients are well blended. Stir in the almonds. Pour the batter into the tube pan. Bake, uncovered, for approximately 45 minutes or until a knife inserted into the center comes out clean. Cool slightly. Invert onto a serving plate.

Glaze:

½	cup sugar
½	cup water
2	tablespoons Cognac

In a small saucepan, heat the sugar and water until the sugar has dissolved. Stir in the Cognac. Cool slightly.

To assemble, spoon the glaze over the warm cake. Cool completely. Store, covered, in the refrigerator or at room temperature.

GREECE

CUSTARD PIE
(Serves 12)

Pastry:

| | non-stick cooking spray |
| 12 | sheets ready-made phyllo pastry |

Prep Time: 35 minutes
Cook Time: 50 minutes

Nutritional Analysis
per serving

Calories	325
Fat	1 g
Sodium	162 mg
Protein	6 g
Carbohydrates	73 g
Cholesterol	4 mg

Preheat oven to 350°. Coat a 1¾ x 7½ x 11¾-inch baking dish with the cooking spray. Place 6 sheets of pastry on the bottom of the dish, coating with spray between each sheet.

Filling:

½	cup sugar
4	cups lowfat milk
1	cup freshly ground bread crumbs
1	cup egg product
2	teaspoons vanilla extract

In a saucepan, mix the sugar, milk and bread crumbs. Cook, stirring constantly, over medium heat for 7 minutes or until slightly thickened. Remove from heat. Cool. Spoon ½ of the warm custard mixture into a bowl. Mix in the egg product and vanilla. Return to the saucepan and blend thoroughly with the other half of the custard.

To assemble, spread the filling evenly over the pastry. Place the remaining pastry on top, coating with spray between layers. Bake, uncovered, for approximately 35 minutes or until the pastry is golden brown.

Syrup:

3	cups sugar
1½	cups water
2	teaspoons vanilla extract
1	tablespoon each lemon juice and grated lemon peel

In a saucepan, mix the sugar and water. Bring to a boil. Cook, uncovered, for 5 minutes, stirring occasionally. Add the vanilla, lemon juice and lemon peel. Reduce heat to medium and cook, stirring occasionally, for 3 minutes longer. While still slightly hot, pour the syrup over the pie. Cool. To serve, cut into squares.

GREECE

Prep Time: 30 minutes
Cook Time: 55-65 minutes

Nutritional Analysis
per serving

Calories	389
Fat	7 g
Sodium	139 mg
Protein	5 g
Carbohydrates	74 g
Cholesterol	0 mg

BAKLAVA

(Serves 12)

Filling:

2	cups finely ground almonds
1	tablespoon ground cloves
3	tablespoons cinnamon

Preheat oven to 350°. In a bowl, mix all ingredients. Set aside.

Pastry:

	non-stick cooking spray
1	pound ready-made phyllo pastry

Coat a 1¾ x 7½ x 11¾-inch baking dish with the spray. Place 4 sheets of pastry into the baking dish. Sprinkle with some of the almond mixture. Continue layering single sheets into the pan, coating each with the spray. Sprinkle the almond mixture evenly between the sheets. Continue until the pastry and almond mixture are gone. Top with a layer of 3 pastry sheets, coating between each. Bake, uncovered, for approximately 45 to 50 minutes or until golden brown. Cool.

Syrup:

3	cups sugar
4	cups water
1	teaspoon vanilla extract
2	tablespoons lemon juice

In a saucepan, bring the sugar, water, vanilla and lemon juice to a boil. Reduce heat to medium and cook, stirring occasionally, for approximately 10 minutes or until slightly thickened. While still slightly hot, pour the syrup over the baklava. To serve, cut into angular pieces.

Facing page — Italy (pictured clockwise): Cappuccino Cheesecake, Chicken Marsala, Sautéed Broccoli, Gnocchi with Tomato Sauce, Bruschetta

ITALY

Beverage Suggestions

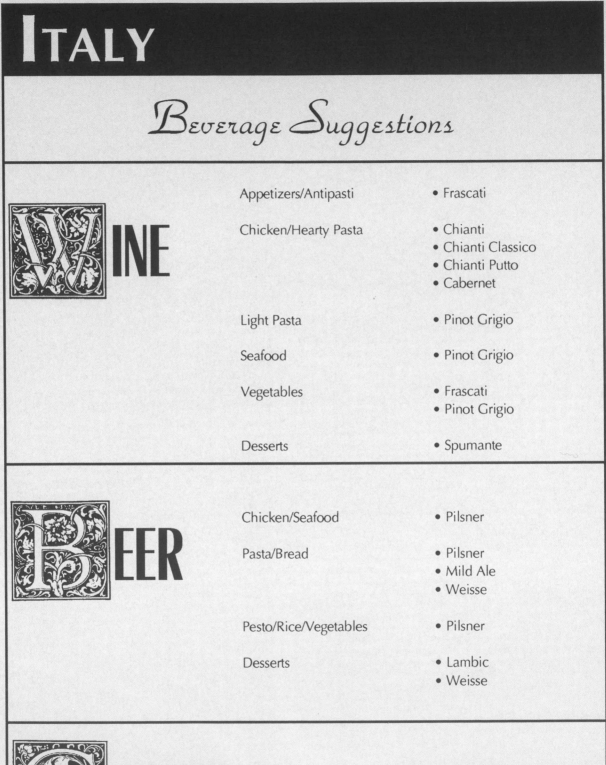

WINE

Appetizers/Antipasti	• Frascati
Chicken/Hearty Pasta	• Chianti • Chianti Classico • Chianti Putto • Cabernet
Light Pasta	• Pinot Grigio
Seafood	• Pinot Grigio
Vegetables	• Frascati • Pinot Grigio
Desserts	• Spumante

BEER

Chicken/Seafood	• Pilsner
Pasta/Bread	• Pilsner • Mild Ale • Weisse
Pesto/Rice/Vegetables	• Pilsner
Desserts	• Lambic • Weisse

COFFEE

Amaretto
Cappuccino
Dark Italian Espresso

ITALY

I t's no secret that Italian cuisine is my favorite. I love the ease of preparing light dishes using fresh herbs, vegetables, seafood and poultry. Italian people are no different — they put so much love and care into the preparation and presentation of their food — and the freshness is of particular importance. Once, when my husband ordered the piccione (pigeon) for his entrée, he asked the waiter if the birds were specifically raised for cooking. The waiter laughed and said, "No signore, you probably played with this pigeon this afternoon in the piazza!"

The wine served in Italy is just as important as the food. For example, Chianti Classico is *the* wine of Florence. Not all wine sold as Chianti is the real thing, however. Only that which is produced in the districts of Florence and Sienna has the right, by law, to be called Chianti Classico. It is a full-bodied, fruity red wine that is worth all the effort it takes to make.

In the Northern city of Genoa, I discovered my favorite Italian sauce — pesto. Using fresh basil blended with garlic, olive oil, Parmesan cheese and pine nuts, the Genoans create a most delicious combination. Since it is the basil which gives pesto its wonderful flavor, I have found that I can omit the cheese and use the oil and nuts sparingly to still create a comparable sauce without all the fat.

What trip to Italy would be complete without a visit to Rome? Although known for its famous veal dishes, I found that I can use chicken instead to produce a lighter version without sacrificing any of the flavor. Chicken Marsala with boneless chicken breasts is every bit as delicious as its veal counterpart.

The Southern regions tend to have the heaviest cuisine. It is here where you find the typical Italian dishes that most Americans recognize. Pizza, Lasagna, Eggplant Parmesan, Spaghetti with Meatballs and all the Italian foods we've grown to enjoy have their roots in and around Naples. Dishes are topped with an abundance of cheeses, meats and sausages. Olive oil is used but, in my opinion, almost to the point of overuse. There's no need for this anymore. *International Light Cuisine* teaches you how to cook wonderful Italian meals that are fresh, flavorful *and* healthy.

ITALY

ARTICHOKE APPETIZER
(Serves 12)

2	16-ounce cans artichoke hearts, drained
4	garlic cloves
1	teaspoon crushed red pepper
½	cup fat-free mayonnaise
2	tablespoons finely chopped parsley

Preheat oven to 350°. In a food processor, combine the artichokes, garlic, red pepper and mayonnaise. Blend until smooth. Transfer the mixture to a baking dish and top with the parsley. Bake, uncovered, for approximately 15 minutes or until slightly browned. Remove from the oven and place on a heat-resistant platter. To serve, surround the dish with fat-free crackers or toasted, thinly sliced French bread.

Prep Time: 15 minutes
Cook Time: 15-20 minutes

Nutritional Analysis
per serving

Calories	37
Fat	0 g
Sodium	136 mg
Protein	1 g
Carbohydrates	7 g
Cholesterol	0 mg

BRUSCHETTA
(Serves 8)

1	loaf Italian bread, cut into ½-inch slices
	non-stick olive oil cooking spray
½	cup finely chopped onion
1	cup finely chopped basil
½	cup finely chopped, seeded, peeled fresh tomatoes
¼	teaspoon crushed red pepper
2	tablespoons olive oil
3	garlic cloves

Preheat oven to 375°. Arrange the bread slices flat on a baking sheet. Coat lightly with the cooking spray. In a bowl, mix the onion, basil, tomato, red pepper and olive oil. Set aside. Bake the bread slices for approximately 10 minutes or until slightly browned. Remove from the oven. Rub the whole garlic cloves across the slices several times. Discard the used cloves. Spread the tomato mixture evenly on each slice. Serve at room temperature.

Bruschetta makes a wonderful appetizer for any Italian meal. Served alone, it is also the perfect light snack.

Prep Time: 15 minutes
Cook Time: 10 minutes

Nutritional Analysis
per serving

Calories	141
Fat	4 g
Sodium	178 mg
Protein	4 g
Carbohydrates	20 g
Cholesterol	0 mg

MUSSELS MARINARA

(Serves 4)

5	garlic cloves, coarsely chopped
½	cup finely chopped onion
2	tablespoons olive oil
½	cup finely chopped parsley
2	cups coarsely chopped, seeded, peeled tomatoes
½	cup white wine
1	teaspoon crushed red pepper
½	teaspoon black pepper
24	large fresh mussels

In a large, shallow pan, sauté the garlic and onion in the olive oil until golden. Add the parsley, tomato, white wine, red pepper, black pepper and mussels. Bring to a boil. Reduce heat to medium and cook, covered, for 20 minutes. Discard any mussels that do not open. To serve, place the mussels into 4 small bowls and spoon the sauce over top.

Really hungry? Make Mussels Marinara your main course by serving it over fresh pasta.

Prep Time: 20 minutes
Cook Time: 25-30 minutes

Nutritional Analysis
per serving

Calories	*506*
Fat	*15 g*
Sodium	*849 mg*
Protein	*58 g*
Carbohydrates	*25 g*
Cholesterol	*128 mg*

ITALY

Prep Time: 20 minutes
Cook Time: 35 minutes

Nutritional Analysis
per serving

Calories   118
Fat   5 g
Sodium   444 mg
Protein   7 g
Carbohydrates   8 g
Cholesterol   14 mg

STUFFED CLAMS

(Makes 24/Serves 6)

Clams:

12	large fresh clams

Preheat oven to 350°. Place the clams into a large pot. Fill the pot ¼ full with water. Cover and bring to a rapid boil. Continue boiling for approximately 10 minutes longer or until the clams open. Discard any that do not. Remove the clams, discarding the cooking liquid. Cool. Take the meat from the shells. Break the shells into halves and set aside. Finely chop the clams.

Stuffing:

1	teaspoon minced garlic
½	cup fine bread crumbs
¼	cup minced celery
1	teaspoon crushed red pepper
1	teaspoon salt
2	tablespoons olive oil
½	cup white wine

In a bowl, mix the clams, garlic, bread crumbs, celery, red pepper, salt, olive oil and wine.

To assemble, place 1 tablespoon of the mixture onto each half shell and arrange on a baking sheet. Bake, uncovered, for approximately 25 minutes or until hot. If the clams appear to be drying out, sprinkle a small amount of water on top of each one.

STUFFED HERB MUSHROOMS
(Makes 24/Serves 8)

Mushrooms:

24	large mushrooms

Clean the mushrooms well. Remove the stems and set the caps aside. In a food processor, mince the stems. Set aside.

Stuffing:

2	garlic cloves, chopped
1	medium onion, chopped
1	teaspoon olive oil
2	cups reduced-calorie bread crumbs (made from reduced-calorie bread)
2	teaspoons chopped oregano
2	teaspoons chopped marjoram
2	teaspoons chopped thyme
2	teaspoons chopped parsley
1	teaspoon crushed red pepper
1	cup defatted chicken stock
1	cup white wine

In a skillet, sauté the garlic, onion and minced mushroom stems in the olive oil until the stems are browned. Add the bread crumbs, oregano, marjoram, thyme, parsley, red pepper and chicken stock. Mix well.

To assemble, place the mushroom caps into a baking dish and stuff with the bread crumb mixture. Pour the wine slowly over the caps. Chill, covered, for 3 hours to overnight. Preheat oven to 350°. Bake, covered, for approximately 15 to 20 minutes. Remove the cover and bake for approximately 10 minutes longer or until the mushrooms are tender and browned.

Prep Time: 20 minutes
Cook Time: 30-35 minutes
Misc Time: Marinate 3 hours
to overnight

Nutritional Analysis
per serving

Calories	*147*
Fat	*3 g*
Sodium	*336 mg*
Protein	*4 g*
Carbohydrates	*22 g*
Cholesterol	*2 mg*

ITALY

CAESAR SALAD
(Serves 8)

Prep Time: 25 minutes

*Nutritional Analysis
per serving*

Calories	140
Fat	9 g
Sodium	452 mg
Protein	3 g
Carbohydrates	10 g
Cholesterol	3 mg

Salad:

2	medium heads Romaine lettuce

Wash and dry the lettuce thoroughly and tear into small pieces. Chill, covered, in the refrigerator until ready for use.

Dressing:

2	garlic cloves, peeled
8	anchovy filets
½	cup worcestershire sauce
½	cup red wine vinegar
¼	cup olive oil
1	tablespoon dijon mustard
2	egg whites
1	medium lemon, freshly squeezed
2	cups toasted croutons

In a large wooden salad bowl, mash the garlic and anchovies with a fork until a paste is formed. Mix in the worcestershire sauce, vinegar and olive oil. Stir until well blended. Add the dijon mustard, egg whites and lemon juice. Blend well. To serve, toss the lettuce and croutons to coat completely with the dressing. Serve immediately.

For a more traditional taste, add ½ cup of fat-free Parmesan cheese and top with freshly ground black pepper.

Pasta Salad with Pesto Sauce
(Serves 8)

Pasta:

    4   cups spiral pasta

In a large pot, cook the pasta until *al dente*. Drain and set aside.

Pesto Sauce:

    2   cups fresh basil leaves
               or 5 tablespoons dried basil
    1   cup fresh parsley
    ½   cup fresh chives
               or 4 teaspoons dried chives
    ¼   cup olive oil
    2   garlic cloves

In a food processor, blend the basil, parsley, chives, olive oil and garlic until smooth.

Salad:

    2   cups thinly sliced carrots
    1   cup thinly sliced mushrooms
    1   cup thinly sliced broccoli flowerets
    1   cup pitted and sliced Calamata olives
    ¼   teaspoon black pepper
    ½   teaspoon salt

In a large salad bowl, combine the cooked pasta, carrots, mushrooms, broccoli, olives, black pepper and salt. Pour in the sauce. Mix until well-coated.

Any kind of pasta may be used for pasta salad, but I prefer bite-sized shells and rotini. The addition of parsley and chives makes for an interesting deviation from the classic basil-pesto sauce.

Prep Time: 25 minutes
Cook Time: 20 minutes

Nutritional Analysis
per serving

Calories	*327*
Fat	*10 g*
Sodium	*169 mg*
Protein	*8 g*
Carbohydrates	*50 g*
Cholesterol	*0 mg*

ITALY

CHICKEN WITH BASIL-WINE SAUCE
(Serves 6)

Prep Time: 10 minutes
Cook Time: 10-15 minutes

Nutritional Analysis
per serving

Calories   271
Fat   5 g
Sodium   367 mg
Protein   31 g
Carbohydrates   13 g
Cholesterol   74 mg

6	boneless chicken breasts, pounded thin
1	cup bread crumbs
1	tablespoon olive oil
1½	cups white wine
1	tablespoon finely chopped fresh basil
1	teaspoon minced garlic
½	teaspoon salt
½	teaspoon black pepper

In a large bowl, dredge the chicken breasts in the bread crumbs. In a skillet, sauté the breasts in the olive oil for approximately 6 to 8 minutes or until well browned. Remove to a heated platter. Add the wine, basil and garlic to the hot skillet. Reduce heat to medium and cook for 1 minute longer. Return the chicken to the skillet and allow it to "plump" in the sauce, cooking for approximately 2 minutes. Season with the salt and pepper.

CHICKEN WITH WINE-CAPER SAUCE
(Serves 8)

Prep Time: 10 minutes
Cook Time: 15 minutes

Nutritional Analysis
per serving

Calories   170
Fat   4 g
Sodium   420 mg
Protein   29 g
Carbohydrates   1 g
Cholesterol   73 mg

8	boneless chicken breasts, pounded thin
1	tablespoon olive oil
½	cup white wine
¼	cup capers with juice
¼	cup lemon juice
1	teaspoon salt
1	teaspoon black pepper
	lemon slices for garnish

In a skillet, sauté the chicken breasts in the olive oil for approximately 10 minutes or until well browned. Remove to a heated platter. Add the wine, capers, lemon juice, salt and pepper to the skillet. Cook over medium heat for 1 minute. Pour the sauce over the chicken. Garnish with lemon slices.

CHICKEN CACCIATORA

(Serves 8)

6	garlic cloves, minced
2	large yellow onions, peeled, thinly sliced
2	tablespoons olive oil
12	chicken breasts, skinned, cut into halves
2	green bell peppers, seeded, julienned
1	cup thickly sliced mushrooms
3	cups coarsely chopped, seeded, peeled tomatoes
1	cup finely chopped parsley
2	tablespoons crushed oregano
1	teaspoon crushed red pepper
1	cup dry red wine
½	teaspoon salt

Prep Time: 25 minutes
Cook Time: 45-50 minutes

Nutritional Analysis
per serving

Calories	*309*
Fat	*7 g*
Sodium	*244 mg*
Protein	*44 g*
Carbohydrates	*9 g*
Cholesterol	*110 mg*

In a large, deep skillet, sauté the garlic and onion in the olive oil until golden. Add the chicken. Cook for approximately 10 minutes or until well browned. Add the green pepper and mushrooms. Mix well. Add the tomato, parsley, oregano and crushed red pepper. Bring to a medium boil. Add the wine and salt. Reduce heat and simmer, partially covered, for approximately 25 to 30 minutes or until the chicken is tender.

My family enjoys Chicken Cacciatora when served with pasta although it can also be served over rice.

ITALY

CHICKEN MARSALA

(Serves 8)

Prep Time: 15 minutes
Cook Time: 15 minutes

Nutritional Analysis
per serving

Calories	*219*
Fat	*6 g*
Sodium	*430 mg*
Protein	*30 g*
Carbohydrates	*9 g*
Cholesterol	*73 mg*

8	boneless chicken breast halves, pounded thin
½	cup all-purpose flour
2	tablespoons olive oil
2	garlic cloves, minced
1	tablespoon minced onion
½	cup coarsely chopped parsley
½	teaspoon black pepper
1	pound mushrooms, thinly sliced
2	cups sweet Marsala wine

In a large bowl, dredge the chicken breasts in flour on both sides. In a large skillet, sauté the chicken in the olive oil over medium heat for approximately 6 to 8 minutes or until well browned. Remove to a heated platter. Add the garlic, onion, parsley, pepper and mushrooms to the pan. Cook, stirring often, for approximately 3 minutes or until the mushrooms begin to brown. Add the Marsala wine. Cook for 1 minute longer. Return the chicken to the pan. Cook in the wine sauce for approximately 2 minutes. Serve immediately.

ITALY

CHICKEN PICCATA
(Serves 8)

8	boneless chicken breast halves, pounded thin
1	cup fine bread crumbs
2	tablespoons olive oil
2	garlic cloves, minced
1	pound mushrooms, thinly sliced
½	cup coarsely chopped parsley
½	teaspoon black pepper
¾	cup freshly squeezed lemon juice
½	cup dry white wine

In a large bowl, dredge the chicken in the bread crumbs. In a large skillet, sauté the chicken in the olive oil over medium heat for approximately 6 to 8 minutes or until well browned. Remove to a heated platter. Add the garlic, mushrooms, parsley and pepper to the pan. Cook, stirring often, until the mushrooms begin to brown. Add the lemon juice and wine. Cook for 1 minute longer. Return the chicken to the pan. Cook in the sauce for approximately 2 minutes. Serve immediately.

Prep Time: 15 minutes
Cook Time: 15-20 minutes

Nutritional Analysis
per serving

Calories	*254*
Fat	*6 g*
Sodium	*159 mg*
Protein	*31 g*
Carbohydrates	*14 g*
Cholesterol	*74 mg*

ITALY

LEMON CHICKEN WITH ARTICHOKES

(Serves 8)

Prep Time: 15 minutes
Cook Time: 15-20 minutes

Nutritional Analysis
per serving

Calories	*190*
Fat	*4 g*
Sodium	*93 mg*
Protein	*29 g*
Carbohydrates	*5 g*
Cholesterol	*73 mg*

1	tablespoon olive oil
2	garlic cloves, minced
8	boneless chicken breasts, pounded thin
8	canned artichoke hearts, sliced medium
1	medium lemon, freshly squeezed
½	cup white wine
2	teaspoons freshly ground black pepper
½	cup finely chopped parsley

In a skillet, sauté the garlic in the olive oil until golden. Add the chicken. Cook for approximately 6 to 8 minutes or until well browned. Remove to a heated platter. Add the artichokes. Sauté until slightly browned. Add the lemon juice, wine, pepper and parsley. Return the chicken to the skillet and allow it to "plump" in the sauce, cooking for approximately 2 minutes. Serve immediately.

Pesto Chicken over Angel Hair

(Serves 8)

Pesto Sauce:

4	garlic cloves
2	cups fresh basil leaves
1	tablespoon pine nuts
¼	cup olive oil
1	teaspoon black pepper

In a food processor, blend all ingredients until smooth. Set aside.

Chicken:

2	boneless chicken breasts
1	garlic clove, minced
1	tablespoon olive oil
	pesto sauce (see above)
½	teaspoon crushed red pepper
1	cup thinly sliced mushrooms
½	cup dry white wine

Trim the boneless chicken breasts of all fat, pound well and cut into very thin strips. In a skillet, sauté the garlic in the olive oil until golden. Add the chicken. Sauté for approximately 6 to 8 minutes or until well browned. Remove the chicken to a heated platter. Add the pesto sauce, red pepper, mushrooms and wine to the skillet. Cook for 5 minutes longer over medium heat. Return the chicken to the skillet. Mix with the sauce until well coated.

Pasta:

1	pound angel hair pasta

In a large pot, cook the pasta until *al dente*. Drain. Serve on individual plates and spoon the chicken and sauce over top.

Prep Time: 25 minutes
Cook Time: 30 minutes

Nutritional Analysis
per serving

Calories	*252*
Fat	*10 g*
Sodium	*167 mg*
Protein	*18 g*
Carbohydrates	*20 g*
Cholesterol	*37 mg*

ITALY

Prep Time: 25 minutes
Cook Time: 25 minutes

Nutritional Analysis
per serving

Calories	*523*
Fat	*8 g*
Sodium	*42 mg*
Protein	*22 g*
Carbohydrates	*85 g*
Cholesterol	*18 mg*

LINGUINE WITH CLAM SAUCE

(Serves 4)

Sauce:

5	garlic cloves, coarsely chopped
$\frac{1}{2}$	cup finely chopped onion
2	tablespoons olive oil
$\frac{1}{2}$	teaspoon crushed red pepper
$\frac{1}{2}$	cup finely chopped parsley
1	cup coarsely chopped, seeded, peeled tomatoes
24	fresh little neck clams in the shell
$\frac{1}{2}$	cup white wine

In a large, shallow pan, sauté the garlic and onion in the olive oil until golden. Add the red pepper, parsley, tomato, clams and wine. Bring to a boil. Reduce heat to medium and cook, covered, for approximately 5 minutes or until the clam shells open. Discard any that do not.

Pasta:

1	pound linguine

In a large pot, cook the linguine until *al dente*. Drain. Serve on individual plates with 6 clams on each bed of pasta. Spoon the sauce over top.

To make a delicious white clam sauce, simply omit the tomatoes.

PASTA WITH TUNA AND CAPERS
(Serves 4)

Sauce:

2	garlic cloves, minced
½	cup finely chopped onion
1	tablespoon olive oil
2	cups chopped, seeded, peeled tomatoes
½	cup chopped parsley
2	tablespoons capers
½	cup white wine
1	cup coarsely flaked water-packed tuna

In a skillet, sauté the garlic and onion in the olive oil until golden. Add the tomato, parsley, capers and wine. Cook over high heat for 5 minutes. Reduce heat and simmer, uncovered, for 15 minutes. Add the tuna and cook for 2 minutes longer. Do not stir the sauce too much as tuna tends to disintegrate.

Pasta:

1	pound pasta (angel hair, linguine or spaghetti)

In a large pot, cook the pasta until *al dente*. Drain. Serve on individual plates and ladle the sauce over top.

Prep Time: 25 minutes
Cook Time: 35-40 minutes

Nutritional Analysis
per serving

Calories	285
Fat	5 g
Sodium	304 mg
Protein	15 g
Carbohydrates	41 g
Cholesterol	13 mg

RISOTTO FRUTTI DI MARE

(Serves 4)

Prep Time: 25 minutes
Cook Time: 40-45 minutes

Nutritional Analysis
per serving

Calories	*971*
Fat	*15 g*
Sodium	*887 mg*
Protein	*92 g*
Carbohydrates	*91 g*
Cholesterol	*314 mg*

5	garlic cloves, minced
1	cup finely chopped onion
2	teaspoons crushed red pepper
2	tablespoons olive oil
2	cups white wine
2½	cups converted white rice
2	cups coarsely chopped, peeled tomatoes
2	cups fish stock or clam juice
2	cups water
1	pound fresh mussels
1	pound little neck clams
1	pound large shrimp
1	cup chopped parsley

In a skillet, sauté the garlic, onion and red pepper in the olive oil until golden. Add 1 cup of the wine. Bring to a boil. Reduce heat to medium. Add the rice, tomato, fish stock and water. Cook, partially covered for approximately 15 minutes or until ⅔ of the liquid has been absorbed. Peel and devein the shrimp, leaving the tails intact. Add the seafood, parsley and remaining wine to the skillet. Cook, partially covered, for approximately 20 minutes or until all of the liquid has been absorbed, the shrimp turn pink, and the mussels and clams have opened. Discard any that do not.

SHRIMP WITH OREGANO

(Serves 8)

48	large shrimp
5	large garlic cloves, minced
½	cup finely chopped onion
1	tablespoon olive oil
½	cup minced fresh oregano
	or 2 tablespoons dried oregano
1	teaspoon crushed red pepper
1	cup white wine

Peel and devein the shrimp, leaving the tails intact. In a skillet, sauté the garlic and onion in the olive oil until golden. Add the shrimp. Cook, stirring frequently, over medium heat for approximately 5 minutes or until pink and barely golden. Add the oregano, red pepper and wine. Cook for 3 minutes longer. Serve hot.

Prep Time: 40 minutes
Cook Time: 10 minutes

Nutritional Analysis
per serving

Calories	*89*
Fat	*4 g*
Sodium	*199 mg*
Protein	*9 g*
Carbohydrates	*2 g*
Cholesterol	*65 mg*

ITALY

TUNA WITH LEMON–BASIL SAUCE

(Serves 6)

Prep Time: 15 minutes
Cook Time: 15-20 minutes

Nutritional Analysis
per serving

Calories   202
Fat   3 g
Sodium   233 mg
Protein   37 g
Carbohydrates   3 g
Cholesterol   65 mg

6	4-ounce tuna filets
1	tablespoon olive oil
2	tablespoons finely chopped onion
½	cup freshly squeezed lemon juice
½	cup white wine
1	tablespoon chopped fresh basil
1	large tomato, peeled, chopped
½	teaspoon salt
½	teaspoon black pepper
	lemon slices for garnish
	fresh basil leaves for garnish

In a skillet, sauté the tuna filets in the olive oil for approximately 3 to 5 minutes or until slightly browned. Remove to a heated platter. In the same skillet, sauté the onion until golden. Add the lemon juice, wine, basil and tomato. Cook over medium heat for 2 minutes. Return the tuna to the skillet and cover with the sauce. Continue cooking for 5 minutes longer. Season with the salt and pepper. Garnish with lemon slices and fresh basil leaves.

GNOCCHI WITH TOMATO SAUCE

(Serves 6)

Prep Time: 1¼ hours
Cook Time: 60-65 minutes

Nutritional Analysis
per serving

Calories   476
Fat   4 g
Sodium   39 mg
Protein   12 g
Carbohydrates   93 g
Cholesterol   less than 1 mg

Mashed Potatoes:

2	cups cubed, peeled white potatoes
½	cup skim milk
1½	teaspoons olive oil

In a large pot, bring water to a boil. Add the potatoes. Reduce heat to medium-high and cook, partially covered, for approximately 20 minutes or until tender. Drain. Return the potatoes to the pot. Add the milk and olive oil. Whip until creamy.

continued on next page

GNOCCHI (CONTINUED)

Gnocchi:

	mashed potatoes	
5	cups all-purpose flour	
1	egg white	

In a bowl, combine the mashed potatoes, flour and egg white. Mix well. Knead until smooth. Roll lengthwise on a floured board until 1 inch in diameter. Cut into ¾-inch slices. In a large pot, bring water to a rapid boil. Add the gnocchi. Reduce heat to medium-high and cook, uncovered, for approximately 25 minutes or until it rises to the top. Stir occasionally. The gnocchi should be firm when pierced with a fork. Drain and set aside.

Sauce:

4	garlic cloves, minced
½	cup finely chopped onion
1	tablespoon olive oil
6	large tomatoes, peeled, seeded, coarsely chopped
½	cup finely chopped fresh oregano
	or 2 tablespoons dried oregano
½	cup finely chopped fresh parsley
1	teaspoon crushed red pepper
1	teaspoon black pepper
½	cup white wine
	fresh parsley for garnish

In a skillet, sauté the garlic and onion in the olive oil until golden. Add the tomato, oregano, parsley, red pepper, black pepper and wine. Cook over medium heat for 5 minutes, stirring frequently. Reduce heat and simmer, uncovered, for 10 minutes longer. To serve, place the gnocchi into a large bowl and pour the sauce over top. Garnish with fresh parsley.

ITALY

Prep Time: 35 minutes
Cook Time: 1 hour

Nutritional Analysis
per serving

Calories	340
Fat	7 g
Sodium	782 mg
Protein	33 g
Carbohydrates	35 g
Cholesterol	50 mg

GROUND TURKEY LASAGNA
(Serves 8)

Pasta:

1	pound lasagna noodles
1	teaspoon olive oil

In a large pot, boil the noodles in water and the olive oil until *al dente*. Drain and rinse with cold water. Arrange on paper towels to dry.

Sauce:

1	medium onion, diced
6	garlic cloves, minced
1	tablespoon olive oil
1	pound ground turkey breast
2	28-ounce cans tomatoes, peeled, crushed
½	cup finely chopped parsley
2	teaspoons crushed oregano
1	teaspoon black pepper

Preheat oven to 350°. In a skillet, sauté the onion, garlic and turkey in the olive oil until the turkey is well browned. Add the tomato, parsley, oregano and pepper. Simmer, uncovered, for 20 minutes.

Filling:

16	ounces nonfat cottage cheese
½	cup finely chopped parsley

In a food processor, blend the cottage cheese until smooth. Stir in the chopped parsley.

	non-stick cooking spray
½	cup grated nonfat Parmesan cheese

Coat a 2 x 9 x 13½-inch baking dish with spray. Ladle in ¾ cup sauce. Top with ⅓ noodles. Dot with ½ cottage cheese. Layer ⅓ remaining sauce, ½ remaining noodles and remaining cottage cheese. Layer ½ remaining sauce, remaining noodles and remaining sauce. Top with the Parmesan cheese. Bake for approximately 30 minutes or until hot.

MUSHROOM FETTUCCINE

(Serves 4)

Sauce:

4	garlic cloves, minced
1	small onion, finely chopped
1	tablespoon olive oil
1	pound mushrooms, thinly sliced
½	cup coarsely chopped parsley
1	teaspoon crushed red pepper

In a skillet, sauté the garlic and onion in the olive oil until golden. Add the mushrooms, parsley and red pepper. Cook for approximately 10 minutes or until the mushrooms are well browned.

Pasta:

1	pound fettuccine

In a large pot, cook the fettuccine until *al dente*. Drain. To serve, place the pasta in a serving bowl and toss in the sautéed mushrooms.

Prep Time: 10 minutes
Cook Time: 25 minutes

Nutritional Analysis
per serving

Calories	240
Fat	5 g
Sodium	142 mg
Protein	8 g
Carbohydrates	42 g
Cholesterol	0 mg

PASTA WITH GARLIC AND OLIVE OIL

(Serves 4)

Sauce:

4	large garlic cloves, minced
1	teaspoon crushed red pepper
2	tablespoons parsley
1	teaspoon black pepper
2	tablespoons olive oil

In a skillet, sauté the garlic, red pepper, parsley and black pepper in the olive oil until golden.

Pasta:

1	pound pasta (angel hair, linguine or spaghetti)

In a large pot, cook the pasta until *al dente*. Drain. To serve, place the pasta in a serving bowl and mix with the sauce.

Prep Time: 15 minutes
Cook Time: 25 minutes

Nutritional Analysis
per serving

Calories	233
Fat	7 g
Sodium	3 mg
Protein	6 g
Carbohydrates	36 g
Cholesterol	0 mg

ITALY

Prep Time: 25 minutes
Cook Time: 20-25 minutes

Nutritional Analysis
per serving

Calories	335
Fat	5 g
Sodium	25 mg
Protein	11 g
Carbohydrates	61 g
Cholesterol	0 mg

Pasta Primavera

(Serves 6)

Vegetables:

4	garlic cloves, minced
2	tablespoons olive oil
1	cup broccoli flowerets
1	cup thinly sliced, peeled carrots
½	cup thinly sliced onion
½	cup thinly sliced red bell pepper
1	cup thinly sliced zucchini
1	cup thinly sliced mushrooms
1	teaspoon crushed red pepper
1	teaspoon black pepper

In a skillet, sauté the garlic in the olive oil until golden. Add the broccoli, carrots, onion, red bell pepper, zucchini, mushrooms, crushed red pepper and black pepper. Cook over medium heat for approximately 10 minutes or until the vegetables are tender, but still crispy.

Pasta:

1	pound pasta (fettuccine or linguine)

In a large pot, cook the pasta until al dente. Drain. Serve on individual plates and spoon the vegetables over top.

The beauty and fun of Pasta Primavera is that it may be prepared with any vegetables. So be creative! This is a great opportunity to finally use those veggies that have been lingering in your refrigerator crisper.

PASTA PUTTANESCA
(Serves 8)

Sauce:

2	tablespoons minced garlic
1	cup finely chopped onion
2	tablespoons olive oil
2	anchovy filets, mashed
1	cup white wine
8	cups coarsely chopped, seeded, peeled fresh tomatoes
¾	cup pitted Calamata olives, cut into halves
½	cup capers
1	teaspoon crushed red pepper
1½	cups chopped fresh parsley

In a skillet, sauté the garlic and onion in the olive oil until golden. Mix in the anchovies. Add the wine, tomato, olives, capers and red pepper. Cook, stirring often, over medium heat for approximately 20 minutes or until the sauce has thickened. Stir in the parsley.

Pasta:

1½	pounds pasta (linguine or spaghetti)

In a large pot, cook the pasta until *al dente*. Serve on individual plates and spoon the sauce over top. Serve immediately.

Prep Time: 25 minutes
Cook Time: 35 minutes

Nutritional Analysis
per serving

Calories	*290*
Fat	*10 g*
Sodium	*237 mg*
Protein	*7 g*
Carbohydrates	*40 g*
Cholesterol	*1 mg*

ITALY

Prep Time: 25 minutes
Cook Time: 45 minutes

*Nutritional Analysis
per serving*

Calories	201
Fat	4 g
Sodium	10 mg
Protein	5 g
Carbohydrates	34 g
Cholesterol	0 mg

SPAGHETTI WITH EGGPLANT

(Serves 8)

Sauce:

4	garlic cloves, minced
1	medium onion, finely chopped
1	medium eggplant, unpeeled, coarsely chopped
2	tablespoons olive oil
1	pound coarsely chopped, peeled tomatoes
2	teaspoons crushed oregano
2	teaspoons finely chopped parsley
1	teaspoon crushed red pepper
½	cup white wine

In a skillet, sauté the garlic, onion and eggplant in the olive oil until golden. Add the tomato, oregano, parsley, red pepper and wine. Simmer, uncovered, for 25 minutes.

Pasta:

1½	pounds spaghetti

In a large pot, cook the pasta until *al dente*. Serve on individual plates and spoon the sauce over top.

SPAGHETTI WITH "MEATBALLS"

(Serves 4)

"Meatballs":

1	pound freshly ground turkey breast
1	egg white
2	tablespoons finely chopped parsley
2	tablespoons crushed oregano
2	teaspoons black pepper

Preheat oven to 350°. Mix all ingredients and shape into 1½-inch balls. Bake for approximately 10 minutes or until slightly browned.

Sauce:

4	garlic cloves, minced
1	cup finely chopped onion
1	tablespoon olive oil
4	cups coarsely chopped canned tomatoes
1	teaspoon crushed red pepper
½	cup white wine
1	cup finely chopped parsley
2	tablespoons crushed oregano
½	teaspoon black pepper

In a skillet, sauté the garlic and onion in the olive oil until golden. Add the tomato, red pepper, wine, parsley, oregano and black pepper. Bring the sauce to a rapid boil for 5 minutes, stirring frequently. Add the "meatballs". Reduce heat and simmer, partially covered, for 20 minutes longer.

Pasta:

1	pound spaghetti

In a large pot, cook the spaghetti until *al dente*. Serve on individual plates and top with the "meatballs" and sauce.

Prep Time: 45 minutes
Cook Time: 50 minutes

Nutritional Analysis
per serving

Calories	*514*
Fat	*9 g*
Sodium	*675 mg*
Protein	*45 g*
Carbohydrates	*55 g*
Cholesterol	*87 mg*

ITALY

Prep Time: 10 minutes
Cook Time: 20 minutes

Nutritional Analysis
per serving

Calories	*39*
Fat	*less than 1 g*
Sodium	*32 mg*
Protein	*2 g*
Carbohydrates	*7 g*
Cholesterol	*0 mg*

SAUTÉED BROCCOLI

(Serves 4)

	non-stick olive oil cooking spray
5	garlic cloves, coarsely chopped
½	teaspoon crushed red pepper
1	pound thinly sliced fresh broccoli flowerets

Coat a skillet with the cooking spray. Add the garlic and red pepper. Sauté over medium-high heat until the garlic begins to sizzle. Add the broccoli. Reduce heat to medium and sauté for approximately 15 minutes longer or until tender and slightly browned.

Prep Time: 10 minutes
Cook Time: 20 minutes

Nutritional Analysis
per serving

Calories	*171*
Fat	*2 g*
Sodium	*19 mg*
Protein	*4 g*
Carbohydrates	*34 g*
Cholesterol	*0 mg*

RISI E BISI

(Serves 6)

3	cups water
2	cups converted white rice
1	cup green peas (fresh or frozen)
1	tablespoon olive oil
1	teaspoon crushed red pepper
½	cup finely chopped parsley

In a saucepan, bring the water to a boil. Add the rice. Boil for 10 minutes. Add the peas. Reduce heat to medium and cook, partially covered, for 10 minutes longer or until all of the water has been absorbed and the rice is tender. Place in a serving bowl and mix in the olive oil, red pepper and parsley.

HERB BREAD

(Serves 12)

¼	cup olive oil
2	teaspoons finely chopped fresh marjoram
1	tablespoon finely chopped parsley
1	tablespoon finely chopped chives
2	teaspoons crushed oregano
1	teaspoon crushed thyme
1	loaf bread (French or Italian)

In a bowl, mix the olive oil, marjoram, parsley, chives, oregano and thyme. Marinate, covered, in the refrigerator for at least 30 minutes. Preheat oven to 350°. Cut the bread into halves lengthwise. Brush the herb mixture on the cut sides. Bake, uncovered, for approximately 15 to 20 minutes or until the bread is slightly browned.

Prep Time: 15 minutes
Cook Time: 15-20 minutes
Misc Time: Marinate 30 minutes

Nutritional Analysis
per serving

Calories	*140*
Fat	*6 g*
Sodium	*203 mg*
Protein	*3 g*
Carbohydrates	*18 g*
Cholesterol	*0 mg*

ITALY

Prep Time: 25 minutes
Cook Time: 50 minutes
Misc Time: Chill 4 hours
*   to overnight*

Nutritional Analysis
per serving

Calories	*250*
Fat	*1 g*
Sodium	*87 mg*
Protein	*3 g*
Carbohydrates	*42 g*
Cholesterol	*less than 1 mg*

CAPPUCCINO CHEESECAKE

(Serves 12)

Crust:

	non-stick cooking spray
1	cup plain lowfat chocolate cookie crumbs
1½	teaspoons ground cinnamon
1	large egg white

Preheat oven to 350°. Coat a 9-inch springform pan with the spray. In a bowl, mix the cookie crumbs, cinnamon and egg white with a fork. Press onto the bottom of the pan. Bake for 10 minutes. Cool.

Filling:

16	ounces lowfat ricotta cheese
6	ounces lowfat cream cheese, softened
¾	cup nonfat plain yogurt
1½	cups sugar
½	cup all-purpose flour
5	teaspoons espresso coffee powder
1	tablespoon vanilla extract

In a food processor, purée the ricotta cheese. Add the cream cheese, yogurt, sugar and flour. Blend well. In a cup, mix the coffee powder and vanilla. Add to the cheese mixture. Process for 20 seconds or until well blended.

To assemble, pour the filling over the pan crust. Bake, uncovered, for approximately 40 minutes or until set in the center. Cool completely. Chill, covered, for 4 hours to overnight.

Topping:

½	cup plain lowfat chocolate cookie crumbs
	lowfat whipped topping for garnish
	chocolate-covered coffee beans for garnish

To serve, remove the side of the springform pan. Pat the cookie crumbs around the side of the cheesecake. Garnish with the whipped topping and coffee beans.

FRUIT GELATI

There is no more satisfying way to end a delightful meal than with a light, fresh fruit gelato or Italian ice. This dessert can be made very simply by using an ice cream freezing unit. Any kind of fruit may be puréed and frozen into this special treat.

SIMPLE SYRUP

(Makes 2½ cups)

2	cups water
1½	cups sugar

In a saucepan, warm the water and sugar over medium heat until the sugar has dissolved. Cool. Store, covered, in the refrigerator until ready for use.

Cook Time: 5 minutes

Nutritional Analysis is included in each gelato recipe that follows.

CANTALOUPE GELATO

(Serves 6)

2	cups chopped cantaloupe
1	cup Simple Syrup, cooled (see above)

In a food processor, purée the cantaloupe until liquified. Chill the bowl of the ice cream freezer. Add the Simple Syrup and cantaloupe purée to the bowl. Churn until frozen (approximately 25 minutes or according to the individual freezing unit).

Prep Time: 40 minutes

Nutritional Analysis per serving

Calories	91
Fat	0 g
Sodium	5 mg
Protein	less than 1 g
Carbohydrates	22 g
Cholesterol	0 mg

CHAMPAGNE GELATO

(Serves 6)

2	cups dry champagne
1	cup Simple Syrup, cooled (see above)

Chill the bowl of the ice cream freezer. Add the champagne and Simple Syrup to the bowl. Churn until frozen (approximately 25 minutes or according to the individual freezing unit).

Prep Time: 35 minutes

Nutritional Analysis per serving

Calories	127
Fat	0 g
Sodium	6 mg
Protein	less than 1 g
Carbohydrates	19 g
Cholesterol	0 mg

ITALY

Prep Time: 40 minutes

Nutritional Analysis per serving

Calories	92
Fat	0 g
Sodium	6 mg
Protein	less than 1 g
Carbohydrates	23 g
Cholesterol	0 mg

HONEYDEW GELATO
(Serves 6)

2   cups chopped honeydew melon
1   cup Simple Syrup, cooled (see page 101)

In a food processor, purée the honeydew until liquified. Chill the bowl of the ice cream freezer. Add the Simple Syrup and honeydew purée to the bowl. Churn until frozen (approximately 25 minutes or according to the individual freezing unit).

Prep Time: 40 minutes

Nutritional Analysis per serving

Calories	134
Fat	less than 1 g
Sodium	5 mg
Protein	1 g
Carbohydrates	32 g
Cholesterol	0 mg

KIWIFRUIT GELATO
(Serves 6)

8   kiwifruit, peeled, cut into halves
1   teaspoon lemon juice
1   cup Simple Syrup, cooled (see page 101)

In a food processor, purée the kiwifruit and lemon juice until liquified. Chill the bowl of the ice cream freezer. Add the Simple Syrup and the kiwifruit purée to the bowl. Churn until frozen (approximately 25 minutes or according to the individual freezing unit).

Prep Time: 40 minutes

Nutritional Analysis per serving

Calories	109
Fat	0 g
Sodium	1 mg
Protein	1 g
Carbohydrates	27 g
Cholesterol	0 mg

ORANGE GELATO
(Serves 6)

2   cups freshly squeezed orange juice
1   cup Simple Syrup, cooled (see page 101)

Chill the bowl of the ice cream freezer. Add the orange juice and Simple Syrup to the bowl. Churn until frozen (approximately 25 minutes or according to the individual freezing unit).

WATERMELON GELATO

(Serves 6)

2	cups watermelon pieces, seeds removed
1	cup Simple Syrup, cooled (see page 101)

In a food processor, purée the watermelon until liquified. Chill the bowl of the ice cream freezer. Add the Simple Syrup and watermelon purée to the bowl. Churn until frozen (approximately 25 minutes or according to the individual freezing unit).

Prep Time: 40 minutes

Nutritional Analysis per serving

Calories	*89*
Fat	*0 g*
Sodium	*1 mg*
Protein	*less than 1 g*
Carbohydrates	*22 g*
Cholesterol	*0 mg*

MACEDONIA DI FRUTTA

(Serves 8)

2	large apples, peeled, seeded
2	large pears, peeled, seeded
1	large orange, peeled, seeded
1	cup seedless red grapes
1	cup seedless green grapes
4	kiwifruit, peeled, thinly sliced
2	tablespoons sugar
½	cup white wine
¼	cup lemon juice

Cut the apples, pears and orange into bite-sized pieces. Place all fruit in a decorative serving bowl. Add the sugar, wine and lemon juice. Mix well. Chill, covered, until ready to serve.

The sugar, wine and lemon juice help the fruit to maintain its original fresh color. This is a staple dessert in Italian restaurants and a light ending to a delicious meal.

Prep Time: 35 minutes

Nutritional Analysis per serving

Calories	*142*
Fat	*0 g*
Sodium	*4 mg*
Protein	*1 g*
Carbohydrates	*31 g*
Cholesterol	*0 mg*

ITALY

TIRAMISU

(Serves 8)

Prep Time: 30-35 minutes

*Nutritional Analysis
per serving*

Calories	218
Fat	5 g
Sodium	129 mg
Protein	8 g
Carbohydrates	33 g
Cholesterol	12 mg

10	ounces nonfat ricotta cheese
10	ounces lowfat vanilla yogurt
5	tablespoons sugar
1	teaspoon vanilla extract
5	tablespoons strong liquid coffee
3	tablespoons dark rum
16	large, lowfat vanilla wafers
	or 32 small wafers
2	1-ounce squares semisweet chocolate, grated
1	teaspoon unsweetened cocoa powder

In a food processor, blend the ricotta cheese for approximately 1 minute or until smooth. Add the yogurt, sugar and vanilla. Blend well. In a cup, mix the coffee and rum. Brush the liquid on the tops of the vanilla wafers. In each of 8 goblets, layer 3 tablespoons of the cheese mixture, 1 large vanilla wafer or 2 small vanilla wafers and 1 tablespoon of grated chocolate. Top each with a second vanilla wafer and 3 tablespoons of the cheese mixture. Sprinkle with cocoa powder. Chill, uncovered, until ready to serve.

This is a very typical Italian dessert, but the classic version contains fat-laden cheese and cream. Since Tiramisu translated into English means "pick me up," you'll be picked up much more easily with this lighter adaptation. As another option, lowfat pound cake or angel food cake may be substituted for the vanilla wafers.

Facing page — Spain (pictured clockwise): Marinated Fresh Fruit, Empanadas, Shrimp in Garlic, Black Bean Soup, Eggplant "Caviar", Flan

Beverage Suggestions

 **WINE**

Tapas/Appetizers	• Rioja Blanco
	• Faustino
Poultry	• Rioja Tinto
	• Sangria
Seafood	• Rioja Blanco
	• Faustino
Vegetables	• Fino
Desserts	• Sauterne

 **BEER**

Thick Soup	• Ale
	• Porter
Poultry/Seafood	• Pilsner
Vegetables	• Pilsner
Pastries/Fresh Fruit	• Weisse

 **COFFEE**

Espresso Roast
Rich Colombian Blend

SPAIN

The food of Spain really defies its reputation — it's not as spicy as some may lead you to believe. In fact, Spaniards enjoy using very little spice, opting instead for fresh herbs to enhance the main ingredients in their recipes. Spain's cuisine is as unique as its regions, all known for one specialty or another.

Because of its location in the south of Spain where the temperature is quite warm, Andalusians require their cuisine to complement the climate. One of the most famous dishes native to Andalusia is a cold soup called Gazpacho. Heading northeast we come to probably one of the most popular regions of Spain — Valencia. It is from this area that the better known Spanish cuisine originates. Chicken and Yellow Rice and Paella Valenciana are well-known throughout the world as being native to this area. The abundance of rice and a pungent spice called saffron contribute greatly to their unique flavors.

Off to Barcelona in the region of Catalonia where restaurants offer specials on the freshest of what's in season — the summer months bring out an abundance of bigger-than-life fruits, vegetables and a variety of shellfish. Fall and winter please the palate with the gamey taste of fresh quail and other delightful types of fowl. One of the unique characteristics of Catalonian cuisine is that the recipes have been passed down from generation to generation without significant changes. I guess they know our old adage too, "If it ain't broke..."

Lastly, no trip to Spain would be complete without a visit to Madrid. A popular way to eat there is nibbling on *tapas*, a word which literally means lid. I discovered that the first tapas were pieces of bread used to cover wine glasses to keep out the flies. It wasn't long before people began to nibble on these pieces while drinking their wine — only to discover the pleasure of snacking while drinking. We, in the United States, would consider tapas the equivalent of appetizers. In Spain, it's a whole lot more — and it doesn't just include bread. There are actually tapas bars on many street corners where patrons stop in for a drink in the evening, sample an array of items and skip dinner altogether. It's economical, filling and best of all, delicious. In our country, tapas has also become quite popular. Remember, I've adapted these recipes to be lighter than what you would find in your travels, or for that matter, most restaurants here at home. So, go ahead — be creative *and* healthy, the international way.

SPAIN

MARINATED ARTICHOKES

(Serves 12)

Prep Time: 20 minutes
Misc Time: Marinate 3 hours
            to overnight

Nutritional Analysis
per serving

Calories   56
Fat   2 g
Sodium   40 mg
Protein   1 g
Carbohydrates   8 g
Cholesterol   0 mg

24	canned artichoke hearts, cut into halves
2	tablespoons olive oil
1/3	cup lemon juice
2	tablespoons white wine vinegar
1/2	cup finely chopped onion
1	teaspoon minced garlic
1	bay leaf
1	teaspoon whole black peppercorns

Place the artichokes into a storage bowl. In a separate bowl, mix the remaining ingredients and pour over the artichokes. Stir gently. Marinate, covered, in the refrigerator for 3 hours to overnight. Remove the marinated artichokes from the storage bowl and arrange them in a tapas or other serving dish.

EGGPLANT "CAVIAR"

(Serves 12)

Prep Time: 25 minutes
Cook Time: 30-35 minutes
Misc Time: Chill 3 hours
            to overnight

Nutritional Analysis
per serving

Calories: 72
Fat   2 g
Sodium   70 mg
Protein   2 g
Carbohydrates   12 g
Cholesterol   0 mg

2	large eggplant
2	garlic cloves
1	small onion, cut into halves
1	tablespoon olive oil
1/4	cup lemon juice
3	drops hot pepper sauce
24	1/4-inch thick slices French bread, toasted

Preheat oven to 350°. On an uncoated baking sheet, bake the eggplant whole for approximately 30 to 35 minutes or until very soft. Remove from the oven and cool. Split the eggplant into halves, remove the pulp and discard the skin. Place the pulp in a food processor. Add the garlic cloves, onion, olive oil, lemon juice and hot pepper sauce. Process for 2 minutes or until all ingredients are well blended. Chill, covered, for 3 hours to overnight. To serve, spoon the "caviar" into a bowl and surround it with toasted French bread slices.

MARINATED MUSHROOMS

(Serves 12)

24	medium mushrooms
1	quart water
2	small white onions, thinly sliced
1	garlic clove, minced
$\frac{1}{2}$	cup red wine vinegar
$\frac{1}{2}$	teaspoon salt
1	bay leaf
$\frac{1}{2}$	teaspoon whole black peppercorns
1	tablespoon olive oil

In a saucepan, combine the mushrooms and water. Bring to a boil. Reduce heat and simmer, uncovered, for approximately 10 to 15 minutes or until the mushrooms are tender. Drain, reserving the liquid. Place the mushrooms, onion and garlic in a storage bowl. Set aside. In a saucepan, combine the reserved mushroom liquid, vinegar, salt, bay leaf and peppercorns. Bring to a boil. Reduce heat and simmer, uncovered, for 10 minutes. Pour over the vegetables in the container. Mix in the olive oil. Marinate, covered, in the refrigerator for 3 hours to overnight. Discard the bay leaf. To serve, pour the mushrooms and marinade into a dish and offer with toothpicks or cocktail forks.

The flavor of the mushrooms is greatly increased when left to marinate overnight. In fact, they can be stored in the refrigerator for several days which makes for a quick and easy snack.

Prep Time: 25-30 minutes
Cook Time: 20-25 minutes
Misc Time: Marinate 3 hours
to overnight

Nutritional Analysis
per serving

Calories	*20*
Fat	*1 g*
Sodium	*89 mg*
Protein	*1 g*
Carbohydrates	*2 g*
Cholesterol	*0 mg*

SPAIN

EMPANADAS
(Makes 12/Serves 12)

Prep Time: 35 minutes
Cook Time: 35-40 minutes

Nutritional Analysis
per serving

Calories	235
Fat	5 g
Sodium	382 mg
Protein	16 g
Carbohydrates	30 g
Cholesterol	29 mg

Pastry:

4	cups all-purpose flour
3	tablespoons solid vegetable shortening
1	teaspoon salt
	ice water
	non-stick cooking spray
1	egg white
1	tablespoon water

Preheat oven to 350°. In a bowl, mix the flour, shortening and salt until coarse. Gradually add enough ice water to form a soft dough. On a floured board, roll the pastry out to ¼-inch thickness and cut into 4-inch circles. Coat a baking sheet with the cooking spray. Place the pastries on the prepared baking sheet. Set aside. In a bowl, mix the egg white and water. Set aside.

Filling:

	non-stick olive oil cooking spray
1	pound ground turkey
¾	cup minced onion
2	tablespoons ground cumin
½	teaspoon salt
2	teaspoons hot pepper sauce
12	pimento-stuffed green olives, cut into halves

Coat a skillet with the cooking spray. Sauté the turkey and onion over medium heat until well browned, stirring frequently. Add the cumin, salt and hot pepper sauce. Mix well.

To assemble, spoon 1 tablespoon of filling onto each pastry round. Place 2 olive halves in the center. Fold the pastry over and pinch the edges together to form a half circle. Press the edge decoratively with the tines of a fork. Brush with the egg white mixture. Bake, uncovered, for approximately 30 minutes or until golden. Serve warm or cold.

SAVORY PASTRIES

(Makes 24/Serves 12)

Filling:

	non-stick cooking spray
1	pound ground turkey breast
½	cup finely chopped onion
2	garlic cloves, minced
½	cup dark raisins
1	teaspoon ground cinnamon
¼	teaspoon ground cloves
½	cup canned tomato sauce
½	teaspoon salt

Prep Time: 35 minutes
Cook Time: 15-20 minutes

Nutritional Analysis
per serving

Calories	220
Fat	5 g
Sodium	268 mg
Protein	15 g
Carbohydrates	28 g
Cholesterol	29 mg

Coat a large skillet with the cooking spray. Sauté the turkey, onion and garlic over medium heat until well browned. Stir in the raisins, cinnamon, cloves, tomato sauce and salt. Cook until hot. Set aside.

Pastry:

	non-stick cooking spray
3	cups all-purpose flour
3	tablespoons solid vegetable shortening
½	teaspoon salt
	ice water

Preheat oven to 350°. Coat a baking sheet with the cooking spray. In a bowl, mix the flour, shortening and salt with a fork or pastry cutter until coarse. Gradually add enough ice water to form a soft dough. On a floured surface, divide the dough into halves and roll each half into a 9 x 12-inch rectangle.

To assemble, spread ½ of the filling over the dough. Starting with the long side, roll "jelly-roll" fashion and moisten the edge with water. Tuck in the ends and pinch to seal. Cut into 1-inch slices and place, filling-side up, on the prepared baking sheet. Repeat with the remaining dough and filling. Bake, uncovered, for 15 to 20 minutes or until slightly browned. Serve warm or at room temperature.

SPAIN

Prep Time: 35 minutes
Cook Time: 2-2½ hours
Misc Time: Soak 2 hours

Nutritional Analysis
per serving

Calories   163
Fat   1 g
Sodium   7 mg
Protein   8 g
Carbohydrates   29 g
Cholesterol   0 mg

BLACK BEAN SOUP

(Serves 8)

1	pound dried black turtle beans
4	large garlic cloves, minced
1	large onion, finely chopped
1	large green bell pepper, finely chopped
1	large red bell pepper, finely chopped
1	teaspoon olive oil
2	quarts water
4	tablespoons crumbled bay leaves
1	teaspoon crushed red pepper
2	teaspoons black pepper

In a pot, add enough water to cover the beans. Soak for 2 hours. Discard any that float to the top. Drain and set aside. In a large pot, sauté the garlic, onion and bell pepper in the olive oil until the garlic is golden. Add the water. Bring to a boil. Add the beans and bay leaves. Reduce heat to medium and cook, partially covered, for approximately 2 hours or until tender, stirring occasionally. Add more water if the beans are drying out before they are fully cooked. Stir in the crushed red pepper and black pepper. Discard the bay leaves. Remove 1 cup of the cooked beans and purée in a food processor or blender. Return the purée to the pot. Mix well.

Black Bean Soup is good enough to be served alone or over white rice. Try a touch of wine vinegar or chopped onion for extra flavor.

CALDO GALLEGO
(Serves 8)

1	cup dried white beans
½	pound smoked turkey, cubed
10	cups cold water
3	medium potatoes, peeled, cubed
2	cups thinly sliced cabbage
4	turnips, coarsely chopped
	green tops of the turnips, coarsely chopped

In a pot, add enough water to cover the beans. Soak for 4 hours. Discard any that float to the top. Drain. In a large pot, combine the beans, turkey and 10 cups of fresh water. Bring to a boil. Reduce heat and simmer, partially covered, for 2½ to 3 hours, stirring occasionally. Add the potatoes, cabbage, turnips and turnip tops. Simmer for 1 to 1½ hours longer, stirring occasionally. Serve very hot.

This soup is so flavorful because it's cooked slowly over a long period of time. It can be made a day in advance, refrigerated and reheated.

Prep Time: 30 minutes
Cook Time: 4½ hours
Misc Time: Soak 4 hours

Nutritional Analysis
per serving

Calories	150
Fat	less than 1 g
Sodium	432 mg
Protein	11 g
Carbohydrates	25 g
Cholesterol	9 mg

SPAIN

GAZPACHO

(Serves 8)

Prep Time: 30 minutes
Misc Time: Chill 3 hours
          to overnight

Nutritional Analysis
per serving

Calories   32
Fat   1 g
Sodium   280 mg
Protein   1 g
Carbohydrates   5 g
Cholesterol   0 mg

3	garlic cloves, minced
2	teaspoons olive oil
1	cup water
½	teaspoon salt
3	cups coarsely chopped, seeded, peeled ripe tomatoes (canned tomatoes may be substituted)
½	cup chopped, peeled cucumber
¼	cup minced onion
1½	tablespoons red wine vinegar
2½	cups cold water
	chopped tomato for garnish
	sliced cucumber for garnish
	chopped green bell pepper for garnish
	chopped onion for garnish

In a food processor, combine the garlic, olive oil, 1 cup of cold water, salt, tomato and cucumber. Purée for approximately 2 minutes or until all ingredients are well blended. In a large bowl, mix the purée, onion, vinegar and 2½ cups of water. Chill, covered, for 3 hours to overnight. Garnish with any one or a combination of chopped tomato, sliced cucumber, chopped green pepper or chopped onion.

This soup is a refreshing way to begin a meal, especially during the warmer months of the year.

SPAIN

CHICKEN SALTEADO

(Serves 8)

4	garlic cloves, minced
1	teaspoon crushed red pepper
2	tablespoons olive oil
8	boneless chicken breasts, skinned, cut into thin strips
1	large green bell pepper, thinly sliced
1	large red bell pepper, thinly sliced
1	large onion, thinly sliced
1	cup sliced mushrooms
½	cup white wine
2	tablespoons worcestershire sauce
½	cup minced parsley

Prep Time: 35 minutes
Cook Time: 15 minutes

Nutritional Analysis
per serving

Calories	198
Fat	6 g
Sodium	94 mg
Protein	30 g
Carbohydrates	3 g
Cholesterol	73 mg

In a large skillet, sauté the garlic and crushed red pepper in the olive oil until golden. Add the chicken, green pepper, red pepper, onion and mushrooms. Cook over medium heat for approximately 10 minutes or until the chicken is well browned. Add the wine, worcestershire sauce and parsley. Cook for 2 minutes longer. Serve immediately.

POLLO ASADO (ROASTED CHICKEN)

(Serves 8)

2	whole chickens, skinned
1	tablespoon olive oil
2	teaspoons minced garlic
2	tablespoons minced parsley
1	teaspoon crushed thyme
½	teaspoon black pepper
½	cup white wine

Prep Time: 30 minutes
Cook Time: 45 minutes

Nutritional Analysis
per serving

Calories	312
Fat	12 g
Sodium	130 mg
Protein	45 g
Carbohydrates	1 g
Cholesterol	127 mg

Preheat oven to 350°. Cut the chickens into halves and place flesh-side up in a roasting pan. In a bowl, mix the olive oil, garlic, parsley, thyme, pepper and wine. Pour over the chicken. Bake, uncovered, for approximately 45 minutes or until golden brown and cooked through. To serve, cut the chicken into pieces and place on a heated platter.

SPAIN

SPANISH CHICKEN AND RICE
(Serves 6)

Prep Time: 30 minutes
Cook Time: 35-40 minutes

Nutritional Analysis
per serving

Calories	*446*
Fat	*8 g*
Sodium	*710 mg*
Protein	*37 g*
Carbohydrates	*49 g*
Cholesterol	*74 mg*

2	teaspoons minced garlic
1	medium onion, finely chopped
2	tablespoons olive oil
3	chicken breasts, skinned, cut into halves
2	cups converted white rice
2	cups peeled, chopped tomatoes
1	teaspoon crushed thyme
1/4	cup crumbled bay leaves
2	tablespoons coarsely chopped parsley
1/2	teaspoon ground saffron
4	cups defatted chicken stock
1	cup white wine

In a large skillet, sauté the garlic and onion in the olive oil for 1 minute. Add the chicken breasts. Cook over medium heat for approximately 6 to 8 minutes or until well browned. Add the rice, tomato, thyme, bay leaves, parsley, saffron, chicken stock and wine. Bring to a boil. Reduce heat and simmer, partially covered, for approximately 20 minutes or until the rice is tender and the liquid has been absorbed.

You may add more chicken stock if the rice starts to dry out before it is fully cooked.

SPAIN

PAELLA VALENCIANA

(Serves 8)

24	fresh clams
24	fresh mussels
24	large shrimp
4	garlic cloves, minced
1	large onion, finely chopped
1	teaspoon olive oil
8	chicken breast filets, skinned, cut into halves
1	large red bell pepper, cut into small strips
1	large green bell pepper, cut into small strips
4	cups fish stock or clam juice
2	cups water
1	cup white wine
4	cups converted white rice
2	tablespoons saffron
2	bay leaves
1	teaspoon crushed red pepper
2	large tomatoes, peeled, seeded, chopped
	parsley sprigs for garnish
	lemon wedges for garnish

Prep Time: 35 minutes
Cook Time: 45-50 minutes

Nutritional Analysis per serving

Calories	703
Fat	7 g
Sodium	613 mg
Protein	64 g
Carbohydrates	87 g
Cholesterol	157 mg

Wash the clams and mussels. Peel and devein the shrimp, leaving the tails intact. In a large skillet, sauté the garlic and onion in the olive oil until golden. Add the chicken. Cook over medium heat for 6 to 8 minutes or until well browned. Add the bell peppers. Sauté for 2 minutes longer. Pour in the fish stock or clam juice, water, wine and rice. Add the saffron, bay leaves, crushed red pepper and tomato. Bring to a boil. Reduce heat and simmer, partially covered, for approximately 20 minutes or until ½ of the liquid has been absorbed. Stir occasionally. Add the seafood. Cook for approximately 10 minutes longer or until the rice is tender, the shrimp turn pink, and the clams and mussels have opened. Discard any that do not. The Paella should be moist so it is not necessary for all of the liquid to be completely absorbed. Discard the bay leaves. To serve, arrange the chicken and seafood on top of the rice. Garnish with parsley sprigs and lemon wedges.

SPAIN

SHRIMP IN GARLIC

(Serves 8)

Prep Time: 30 minutes
Cook Time: 15 minutes

Nutritional Analysis
per serving

Calories	*167*
Fat	*5 g*
Sodium	*172 mg*
Protein	*24 g*
Carbohydrates	*4 g*
Cholesterol	*174 mg*

2	pounds large shrimp
5	garlic cloves, minced
1	medium onion, coarsely chopped
2	tablespoons olive oil
¼	cup dry white wine
½	cup lemon juice
¼	cup finely chopped parsley
½	teaspoon crushed red pepper

Peel and devein the shrimp, leaving the tails intact. In a skillet, sauté the garlic and onion in the olive oil until golden. Add the shrimp, wine, lemon juice, parsley and red pepper. Cook, uncovered, over medium heat for approximately 10 minutes or until the shrimp turn pink. Do not overcook as the shrimp will become less tender.

STUFFED POMPANO

(Serves 8)

2	pounds whole pompano
	non-stick cooking spray
1	cup minced onion
2	tablespoons minced garlic
½	cup finely chopped celery
1	tablespoon olive oil
4	cups freshly ground bread crumbs
½	cup finely chopped cilantro
½	cup finely chopped parsley
1	cup chopped, seeded, peeled tomatoes
1	cup fish stock or clam juice
1	cup white wine
	lemon slices for garnish
	parsley sprigs for garnish

Prep Time: 35 minutes
Cook Time: 40 minutes

Nutritional Analysis
per serving

Calories	*491*
Fat	*18 g*
Sodium	*506 mg*
Protein	*36 g*
Carbohydrates	*41 g*
Cholesterol	*75 mg*

Preheat oven to 350°. Clean and gut the fish, leaving the heads and tails intact. Coat a baking pan with the cooking spray. In a skillet, sauté the onion, garlic and celery in the olive oil until golden. Add the bread crumbs, cilantro, parsley, tomato and fish stock or clam juice. Mix well. Cook over medium heat for 5 minutes. Stuff an equal amount of the mixture inside each fish. You may need to split the cavity further to hold the stuffing. Place in the prepared pan. Pour the wine over the fish. Bake, covered, for 40 minutes, basting often. Do not overcook. If the pan becomes dry, add more wine and water. To serve, transfer the fish to a heated platter. Remove the heads and tails and discard. Peel the skin off the top side of the fish, remove a filet and place it along with ½ of the stuffing on a plate. Turn the fish over and repeat the same procedure until only the carcass remains. Garnish with lemon slices and parsley sprigs.

SPAIN

Prep Time: 30 minutes
Cook Time: 20 minutes

Nutritional Analysis
per serving

Calories	274
Fat	8 g
Sodium	683 mg
Protein	45 g
Carbohydrates	3 g
Cholesterol	149 mg

GRILLED SEAFOOD WITH PEPPER SAUCE

(Serves 8)

Pepper Sauce:

$1\frac{1}{2}$	teaspoons	minced garlic
1	teaspoon	crushed red pepper
$\frac{1}{2}$	teaspoon	salt
1	small tomato, peeled, seeded, finely chopped	
$\frac{1}{8}$	cup	red wine vinegar
$\frac{1}{4}$	cup	olive oil

In a small bowl, crush the garlic, red pepper and salt with the back of a large spoon. Add the tomato and vinegar. Mash the mixture until a smooth paste is formed. Add the olive oil 1 spoonful at a time until thoroughly blended.

Seafood:

24	large shrimp
24	large sea scallops
24	1½-inch pieces red snapper or grouper
24	1½-inch pieces lobster tail
	pepper sauce (see above)

Preheat grill to a high flame. Peel and devein the shrimp, leaving the tails intact. Arrange the seafood alternately on 8 skewers. Reduce the flame to medium and grill for approximately 20 minutes or until the seafood is thoroughly cooked, but not dry. To serve, remove the seafood from the skewers onto individual plates and spoon the sauce over top.

SPAIN

FLAN

(Serves 8)

1½	cups sugar
4	cups lowfat milk
1	cup egg product
1½	teaspoons vanilla extract

Preheat oven to 350°. In a skillet, melt ¾ cup sugar over low heat until it dissolves and turns into a golden syrup. Pour into a 2-quart baking dish. Tilt to coat the bottom and sides of the dish. Cool for 20 minutes. In a large bowl, beat the remaining sugar, milk, egg product and vanilla, blending well. Pour the custard mixture on top of the cooled syrup. Place the baking dish inside of a larger baking dish or pan which contains 1 inch of water. Bake for approximately 1¼ hours or until a knife inserted in the center comes out clean. Cool. Chill, covered, for 8 hours to overnight. To serve, run a knife around the sides of the baking dish to loosen the flan. Place a serving plate over top and invert the baking dish so that the flan is turned upside-down onto the plate. Serve cold.

Prep Time: 45 minutes
Cook Time: 75-80 minutes
Misc Time: Chill 8 hours to overnight

Nutritional Analysis per serving

Calories	200
Fat	1 g
Sodium	102 mg
Protein	7 g
Carbohydrates	41 g
Cholesterol	5 mg

MARINATED FRESH FRUIT

(Serves 12)

2	cups whole strawberries, stems removed
2	large apples (green, red or yellow)
2	cups green seedless grapes
2	cups red seedless grapes
1	tablespoon sugar
1	cup dry white wine
2	teaspoons lemon juice

Wash all fruit well. Leave the strawberries whole. Cut the unpeeled apples into bite-sized wedges. Remove the stems from the grapes. In a bowl, combine the fruit, sugar, wine and lemon juice. Toss lightly. Marinate, covered, in the refrigerator for 1 hour. Spoon into a decorative serving bowl.

Prep Time: 20 minutes
Misc Time: Marinate 1 hour

Nutritional Analysis per serving

Calories	78
Fat	0 g
Sodium	2 mg
Protein	less than 1 g
Carbohydrates	15 g
Cholesterol	0 mg

SPAIN

RICE PUDDING
(Serves 8)

Prep Time: 25 minutes
Cook Time: 1 hour

Nutritional Analysis
per serving

Calories	224
Fat	1 g
Sodium	90 mg
Protein	7 g
Carbohydrates	46 g
Cholesterol	29 mg

	non-stick cooking spray
4	cups skim milk
¾	cup long grain white rice
½	cup raisins
1	egg yolk
3	egg whites
½	cup sugar
1	teaspoon vanilla extract
3	teaspoons ground cinnamon
3	teaspoons ground nutmeg
½	cup packed dark brown sugar

Preheat oven to 325°. Coat a 1¾ x 7½ x 11¾-inch baking dish with the cooking spray. In a saucepan, bring 2 cups of the milk, rice and raisins to a boil. Reduce heat and simmer, covered, for approximately 20 minutes or until the rice is tender. Remove from heat. In a bowl, combine the egg yolk, egg whites, remaining 2 cups of milk, sugar and vanilla. Gradually stir the rice mixture into the egg mixture. Pour into the prepared baking dish. Bake, uncovered, for 25 minutes. Stir well. In a bowl, combine the cinnamon, nutmeg and brown sugar. Sprinkle on top of the pudding. Bake for approximately 15 minutes longer or until a knife inserted in the center comes out clean. Serve warm.

Be especially careful not to overbake the pudding as it will become dry.

Facing page — All American (pictured clockwise): Vegetarian Baked Beans, Cocoa Mint Brownies, Dijon Mustard Potato Salad, Spicy Turkey Burgers, Crudités with Dill Dip

ALL AMERICAN

Beverage Suggestions

WINE

Appetizers	• Chablis
	• Chenin Blanc
Poultry	• Chardonnay
	• Cabernet Sauvignon
Seafood/Vegetables	• Chardonnay
	• Sauvignon Blanc
Chocolate	• Orange Muscat
Apple	• Vintage Port
Fruit	• Sauterne

BEER

Poultry	• Mild Ale
	• Bock
	• Amber Lager
Vegetables	• Pilsner
Bread	• Pale Ale
	• Porter
Desserts	• Weisse
	• Lambic

COFFEE

Chocolate Almond
French Coffee with Chicory (Cajun/Creole)
Hazelnut
Kona Blend

ALL AMERICAN

THANKSGIVING

Thanksgiving is probably my favorite holiday of the year. I grew up in the South, where most holiday meals are traditional, so it's no surprise when I prepare a full-blown Thanksgiving feast for my family and friends. A week or so before the big day, I plan my menu — which is basically the same from year to year. I do like to add a little variety though, just to keep everyone on their toes. I guess it's fair to say that my children don't take kindly to major changes this time of year.

Many of the traditional Thanksgiving dishes are full of fat, sugar, cholesterol and, of course, calories. By the end of the meal, even those who have only moderately indulged feel like stuffed turkeys themselves. Nowadays, you don't have to end the meal this way. Over the years, I've learned to convert the standard recipes into delicious, lowfat dishes which have now become the *new* Thanksgiving tradition in our home. You, too, can enjoy the same dishes you remember from your childhood, but without all the fat.

FOURTH OF JULY

The Fourth of July celebrations I remember while growing up were so special. They consisted of a casual day spent with family and friends playing games, watching fireworks and enjoying an old fashioned barbecue with all the trimmings. There were bigger-than-life cheeseburgers hot off the grill, my grandmother's baked beans flavored with bacon, potato salad full of mayonnaise and whole eggs and homemade ice cream which my brother and I reluctantly took turns churning by hand. Everything always tasted so good, but at the time I didn't concern myself with fat and cholesterol. And neither did anyone else in my family. The Fourth was traditional and we didn't deviate from tradition.

Today, I continue the celebration with a slightly different approach. Of course, I still allow my patriotic spirit to go wild by adorning tables with red, white and blue cloths, small American flags and color-coordinated serving dishes. But the feast is quite a bit different. Instead, I have created lighter versions of some of the most popular dishes normally found at Fourth of July parties and cookouts. It's old fashioned taste with a whole new twist — a *better* tradition for your healthy family.

CRUDITÉS WITH DILL DIP

(Serves 8)

Prep Time: 25 minutes
Misc Time: Chill 4 hours
to overnight

Nutritional Analysis
per serving

Calories	*89*
Fat	*0 g*
Sodium	*99 mg*
Protein	*5 g*
Carbohydrates	*16 g*
Cholesterol	*0 mg*

Vegetables:

4	large carrots
12	green asparagus spears
2	cups cauliflower flowerets

Peel and thinly slice the carrots diagonally. Trim the asparagus to 5-inch strips. Cut the cauliflower into small flowerets.

Dill Dip:

2	cups nonfat sour cream product
2	tablespoons minced dillweed or 2 tablespoons fresh dill
2	teaspoons minced green onion

In a bowl, mix all ingredients. Chill, covered, for 4 hours to overnight. To serve, place the dip into a small bowl in the center of a platter and attractively arrange the crudités around it.

Serve while your hungry guests are waiting for the Grilled Marinated Chicken (see page 129) and Spicy Turkey Burgers (see page 131).

ALL AMERICAN

DIJON MUSTARD POTATO SALAD
(Serves 12)

2	pounds new potatoes
2	garlic cloves, minced
1	teaspoon crushed red pepper
½	cup dijon mustard
1	cup nonfat mayonnaise
½	cup wine vinegar (red or white)
2	tablespoons olive oil
1	cup finely chopped green onion
1	cup finely chopped red bell pepper
1	cup finely chopped green bell pepper
1	cup coarsely chopped parsley
1	tablespoon black pepper
½	teaspoon salt
	parsley sprigs for garnish
	sliced red bell pepper for garnish
	sliced green bell pepper for garnish

Prep Time: 35 minutes
Cook Time: 25 minutes
Misc Time: Chill 8 hours
*   to overnight*

Nutritional Analysis
per serving

Calories	*129*
Fat	*4 g*
Sodium	*575 mg*
Protein	*1 g*
Carbohydrates	*22 g*
Cholesterol	*0 mg*

Scrub and rinse the potatoes. In a large pot, bring water to a boil. Add the potatoes. Reduce heat to medium-high and cook, partially covered, for approximately 25 minutes or until tender. Drain and set aside to cool. In a medium bowl, mix the garlic, red pepper, dijon mustard, mayonnaise, wine vinegar and olive oil. Set aside. Cut the cooled potatoes into small pieces and place in a large bowl. Add the green onions, red pepper, green pepper, parsley, black pepper and salt. Add the mustard mixture and toss until well coated. Chill, covered, for 8 hours to overnight. Add 2 tablespoons of water for desired consistency if the potato salad becomes too thick.

For a beautiful presentation, line a shallow serving bowl alternately with red and white cabbage leaves. Heap the potato salad on top and garnish with parsley sprigs and pepper slices.

ALL AMERICAN

SWEET AND SOUR COLESLAW
(Serves 12)

Prep Time: 40 minutes
Misc Time: Chill 8 hours
*   to overnight*

Nutritional Analysis
per serving

Calories	*79*
Fat	*2 g*
Sodium	*118 mg*
Protein	*1 g*
Carbohydrates	*13 g*
Cholesterol	*0 mg*

1	large head white cabbage
1	large head red cabbage
1	cup thinly sliced onion
2	cups grated carrots
1	tablespoon fennel seed
1	tablespoon sugar
½	cup wine vinegar (red or white)
2	tablespoons olive oil
2	teaspoons black pepper
½	teaspoon salt

Finely shred the cabbages into a large bowl. Mix in the onion, carrots, fennel seed, sugar, wine vinegar, olive oil, pepper and salt. Toss well. Chill, covered, for 8 hours to overnight.

For a decorative touch, line an attractive serving bowl with Chinese cabbage leaves or dark green lettuce leaves. Heap the coleslaw on top and garnish with flower-shaped carrots.

ALL AMERICAN

GRILLED MARINATED CHICKEN
(Serves 12)

Marinade:

2	tablespoons olive oil
6	garlic cloves, minced
1	cup minced onion
2	teaspoons worcestershire sauce
1	cup finely chopped parsley
1	teaspoon crushed red pepper
1	cup white wine
½	cup wine vinegar (red or white)
1	teaspoon crushed thyme

In a large bowl, combine all ingredients.

Chicken:

12	large chicken breasts, skinned

Place the chicken into a large container. Pour in the marinade and coat thoroughly. Marinate, covered, for 8 hours to overnight. Preheat the grill to a high flame. Remove the chicken from the container, reserving the marinade. Reduce the flame to medium and grill for approximately 20 to 25 minutes or until crispy on both sides. Baste occasionally with the marinade.

Cook all chicken slowly to be certain that the inside is cooked through before the outside becomes too brown.

Prep Time: 25 minutes
Cook Time: 20-25 minutes
Misc Time: Marinate 8 hours
*   to overnight*

Nutritional Analysis
per serving

Calories	*206*
Fat	*7 g*
Sodium	*74 mg*
Protein	*29 g*
Carbohydrates	*2 g*
Cholesterol	*73 mg*

ALL AMERICAN

ROAST TURKEY

(Serves 12)

Prep Time: 25 minutes
Cook Time: 3½ hours

Nutritional Analysis
per serving

Calories	489
Fat	7 g
Sodium	305 mg
Protein	102 g
Carbohydrates	2 g
Cholesterol	317 mg

1	12-pound turkey
1	teaspoon poultry seasoning
½	teaspoon salt
½	teaspoon black pepper
1	large orange

Preheat oven to 325°. Remove and discard the giblets and neck from the turkey. Rinse the turkey under cold running water and pat dry. Trim off any excess fat. In a bowl, combine the poultry seasoning, salt and pepper. Sprinkle both the body and neck cavities with ½ of the seasoning mixture. Cut the orange into 8 wedges. Place in the neck and body cavities to absorb the juices and fat. Tuck the legs under the flap of skin around the tail or close the body cavity with skewers and truss. Tuck the wings under the turkey. Place the turkey breast-side up in a shallow roasting pan. Sprinkle with the remaining seasoning mixture. Cover loosely with foil and bake for 2½ hours. Uncover and bake for 1 hour longer or until the juices are clear.

If you choose to serve the turkey with Herb Stuffing (see page 134), eliminate putting the oranges in the cavities and substitute the stuffing mixture. Keep in mind that your baking time will increase. A general rule for roasting stuffed turkeys is 20 minutes per pound.

ALL AMERICAN

SPICY TURKEY BURGERS

(Serves 4)

1	pound ground turkey
½	cup minced onion
2	egg whites
2	tablespoons worcestershire sauce
2	teaspoons crushed red pepper
½	cup finely chopped parsley
½	teaspoon salt
	lettuce for garnish
	sliced tomato for garnish
	sliced onion for garnish

Preheat grill to a high flame. In a bowl, mix all ingredients. Make 4 equal-sized patties. Reduce flame to medium and grill for approximately 20 minutes or until cooked through. Garnish with lettuce, tomato and onion or any other condiments of your choice.

In my opinion, these burgers are so good you'll never miss beef. If you're feeding a crowd, simply double or triple the recipe, adjusting the crushed red pepper to taste.

Prep Time: 25 minutes
Cook Time: 20 minutes

*Nutritional Analysis
per serving*

Calories	*218*
Fat	*5 g*
Sodium	*440 mg*
Protein	*38 g*
Carbohydrates	*3 g*
Cholesterol	*87 mg*

CORN CASSEROLE

(Serves 8)

Prep Time: 25 minutes
Cook Time: 45-50 minutes

Nutritional Analysis
per serving

Calories	*190*
Fat	*3 g*
Sodium	*496 mg*
Protein	*8 g*
Carbohydrates	*32 g*
Cholesterol	*2 mg*

	non-stick cooking spray
1½	tablespoons minced garlic
1	cup minced onion
1	green bell pepper, finely chopped
¼	cup minced pimentos
1	tablespoon olive oil
½	cup skim milk
¾	cup defatted chicken stock
2	cups corn kernels (fresh or frozen)
1½	teaspoons chopped oregano (fresh or dried)
1½	teaspoons dried marjoram leaves
1½	teaspoons black pepper
½	teaspoon salt
2	cups coarsely ground day-old bread crumbs
3	egg whites

Preheat oven to 350°. Coat a 2-quart baking dish with the cooking spray. In a large saucepan, sauté the garlic, onion, green pepper and pimentos in the olive oil until the garlic is golden. Add the milk, chicken stock and corn. Simmer for 5 minutes and remove from heat. Add the oregano, marjoram, pepper and salt. Cool for 5 minutes. Add the bread crumbs and egg whites, stirring until well blended. Spoon into the prepared baking dish. Bake, uncovered, for approximately 35 to 40 minutes or until slightly browned on top. Serve immediately.

ALL AMERICAN

CRANBERRY-ORANGE SAUCE
(Serves 12)

1	pound fresh cranberries
1	cup sugar
1	cup red currant jelly
1	cup water
2	tablespoons grated orange peel

In a medium saucepan, combine the cranberries, sugar, jelly and water. Bring to a boil. Reduce heat and simmer, uncovered, for 15 minutes. Remove from heat. Stir in the orange peel. Chill, covered, for 5 hours to overnight.

Make Cranberry-Orange Sauce several days before serving and store it in the refrigerator.

Prep Time: 10 minutes
Cook Time: 20 minutes
*Misc Time: Chill 5 hours
to overnight*

*Nutritional Analysis
per serving*

Calories	*144*
Fat	*0 g*
Sodium	*7 mg*
Protein	*0 g*
Carbohydrates	*36 g*
Cholesterol	*0 mg*

Herb Stuffing

(Serves 12)

Prep Time: 45 minutes
Cook Time: 1 hour

Nutritional Analysis
per serving

Calories	204
Fat	5 g
Sodium	375 mg
Protein	4 g
Carbohydrates	34 g
Cholesterol	3 mg

	non-stick cooking spray
2	teaspoons olive oil
1½	cups finely chopped celery
2	teaspoons minced shallots
1	cup finely chopped onion
1	teaspoon minced garlic
1	cup coarsely chopped, peeled tart apples
6	cups crumbled Corn Bread (see page 138)
	½ recipe only
3	tablespoons finely chopped fresh parsley
2	tablespoons chopped sage
½	teaspoon salt
1	teaspoon dried thyme
½	teaspoon black pepper
¾	cup water

Preheat oven to 325°. Coat a baking dish with the cooking spray. In a large skillet, sauté the celery, shallots, onion, garlic and apples in olive oil until tender. In a large bowl, combine the Corn Bread, parsley, sage, salt, thyme, pepper and water. Add the sautéed mixture. Spoon into the prepared baking dish. Bake, covered, for approximately 20 minutes or until hot.

Making Herb Stuffing the day before Thanksgiving increases the flavor, but do not stuff the turkey until just before baking. Also, if you choose to stuff the turkey, the fat content will increase due to the extra juices released while baking.

ALL AMERICAN

VEGETABLE KABOBS
(Serves 12)

4	large ears corn (yellow or white)
4	large zucchini
4	large yellow squash
4	large onions, peeled (white or purple)
2	tablespoons olive oil
1	teaspoon black pepper

Preheat grill to a medium flame. Remove the husks and silk from the corn. Trim the ends of the corn, zucchini and squash. Cut each of the vegetables into 24 equal pieces. Cut the onion into wedges and separate into layers. Thread the zucchini, corn and squash alternately onto 12 skewers, placing an onion piece between each vegetable. Be sure that each skewer has 2 pieces of each vegetable. Brush on the olive oil. Grill over a medium flame for approximately 20 minutes or until tender. Season with the pepper. Serve immediately.

Prep Time: 30 minutes
Cook Time: 20 minutes

Nutritional Analysis
per serving

Calories	*110*
Fat	*3 g*
Sodium	*17 mg*
Protein	*2 g*
Carbohydrates	*19 g*
Cholesterol	*0 mg*

VEGETABLE MEDLEY
(Serves 12)

1	pound carrots
1	pound broccoli flowerets
1	pound parsnips
	non-stick cooking spray
2	teaspoons minced garlic
½	teaspoon salt

Preheat oven to 325°. Peel the carrots and thinly slice them diagonally. Cut the broccoli into medium pieces. Peel and thinly slice the parsnips. In separate saucepans, blanch the carrots, broccoli and parsnips for approximately 20 minutes each or until tender. Drain. In a baking/serving dish, arrange the vegetables decoratively. Coat thoroughly with the cooking spray. Sprinkle with the garlic and salt. Bake, covered, for approximately 20 minutes or until very hot.

It may not sound too exciting, but this is actually one of our family favorites at Thanksgiving.

Prep Time: 15 minutes
Cook Time: 40 minutes

Nutritional Analysis
per serving

Calories	*60*
Fat	*0 g*
Sodium	*33 mg*
Protein	*1 g*
Carbohydrates	*13 g*
Cholesterol	*0 mg*

VEGETARIAN BAKED BEANS

(Serves 12)

Prep Time: 25 minutes
Cook Time: 2 hours 35 minutes
Misc Time: Soak 3 hours

Nutritional Analysis
per serving

Calories	*238*
Fat	*less than 1 g*
Sodium	*193 mg*
Protein	*7 g*
Carbohydrates	*52 g*
Cholesterol	*0 mg*

1	pound dried white beans
2	quarts water
1	cup finely chopped green bell pepper
1	cup finely chopped onion
2	cups crushed, peeled, canned tomatoes
½	cup packed dark brown sugar
1	cup maple syrup
2	teaspoons black pepper
½	teaspoon salt

In a large pot, add enough water to cover the beans. Soak for at least 3 hours. Remove any that float to the top. Drain. Add 2 quarts of fresh water to the pot. Bring to a rapid boil. Reduce heat and simmer, partially covered, for approximately 2 hours or until the beans are tender, but not mushy. Drain and rinse in a colander. Place the beans in an oven-proof baking dish. Preheat oven to 350°. Add the green pepper, onion, tomato, brown sugar, maple syrup, pepper and salt. Mix well. Bake, covered, for approximately 35 minutes or until a deep brick color. If the beans become too dry, add water to achieve the desired consistency.

ALL AMERICAN

WHIPPED POTATOES

(Serves 8)

3	pounds white Idaho potatoes, peeled
1	cup lowfat milk
2	teaspoons margarine
½	teaspoon salt
1	teaspoon black pepper

Cut the potatoes into small pieces. In a large pot, bring water to a boil. Add the potatoes. Reduce heat to medium-high and cook, partially covered, for approximately 20 minutes or until tender. Drain. In a large bowl, combine the potatoes, milk, margarine, salt and pepper. Whip at high speed with an electric mixer, potato masher or by hand until smooth.

Prep Time: 30 minutes
Cook Time: 25 minutes

Nutritional Analysis
per serving

Calories	*168*
Fat	*1 g*
Sodium	*158 mg*
Protein	*3 g*
Carbohydrates	*36 g*
Cholesterol	*1 mg*

WILD RICE

(Serves 8)

½	cup finely chopped celery
½	cup finely chopped onion
1	cup thinly sliced small mushrooms
2	teaspoons minced garlic
1	teaspoon olive oil
2	cups long grain white rice
2	cups wild rice
6	cups water
2	teaspoons crushed thyme
½	teaspoon salt
1	teaspoon black pepper

In a large deep pan, sauté the celery, onion, mushrooms and garlic in olive oil until golden. Add the white rice, wild rice, water, thyme, salt and pepper. Bring all ingredients to a vigorous boil. Reduce heat and simmer, partially covered, for approximately 25 to 30 minutes or until the rice is tender and the water has been absorbed. Stir occasionally.

Prep Time: 20 minutes
Cook Time: 35-40 minutes

Nutritional Analysis
per serving

Calories	*275*
Fat	*1 g*
Sodium	*500 mg*
Protein	*6 g*
Carbohydrates	*59 g*
Cholesterol	*0 mg*

ALL AMERICAN

CORN BREAD
(Serves 12)

	non-stick cooking spray
2	cups all-purpose flour
1/3	cup sugar
1½	tablespoons baking powder
1	teaspoon salt
2	cups yellow cornmeal
2	cups skim milk
1	tablespoon solid vegetable shortening
1	egg yolk
2	egg whites

Preheat oven to 400°. Coat a 10 x 15-inch baking dish with spray. In a bowl, sift the flour, sugar, baking powder and salt. Stir in the cornmeal. In a large bowl, combine the milk and shortening. In a third bowl, beat the egg yolk and whites lightly. Stir into the milk mixture. Add the dry ingredients. Mix thoroughly. Pour into the prepared dish. Bake, uncovered, for 35 to 40 minutes or until slightly browned.

Prep Time: 20 minutes
Cook Time: 35-40 minutes

Nutritional Analysis
per serving

Calories	203
Fat	2 g
Sodium	385 mg
Protein	6 g
Carbohydrates	40 g
Cholesterol	18 mg

CORN MUFFINS
(Makes 12/Serves 12)

1	cup all-purpose flour
1/3	cup sugar
1	tablespoon baking powder
1/3	teaspoon salt
1	cup yellow cornmeal
2	egg whites
1	cup skim milk
1/4	cup melted margarine
	non-stick cooking spray

Preheat oven to 350°. In a bowl, sift the flour, sugar, baking powder and salt. Stir in the cornmeal. In another bowl, mix the egg whites, milk and margarine. Add to the dry ingredients. Mix well. Coat muffin cups with spray and fill them ¾ full. Bake, uncovered, for approximately 25 minutes or until slightly browned.

Prep Time: 20 minutes
Cook Time: 25 minutes

Nutritional Analysis
per serving

Calories	138
Fat	4 g
Sodium	221 mg
Protein	3 g
Carbohydrates	23 g
Cholesterol	less than 1 mg

ALL AMERICAN

APPLE TART

(Serves 8)

Pastry:

4	cups all-purpose flour
3	tablespoons solid vegetable shortening
1	tablespoon sugar
	ice water
1	egg white
1	tablespoon water

Preheat oven to 350°. In a bowl, mix the flour, shortening and sugar with a fork or pastry cutter until coarse. Gradually add enough ice water to form a soft dough. Separate into 2 balls. Roll 1 ball out on a floured surface. Fit into a 9-inch tart pan or pie plate. Set the other ball aside until the tart is ready for its top crust. In a bowl, mix the egg white with water. Set aside.

Filling:

1	cup seedless raisins
½	cup rum
4	cups thinly sliced, peeled tart apples
2	tablespoons ground cinnamon
1	teaspoon ground cloves
¾	cup packed brown sugar (light or dark)

In a bowl, soak the raisins in rum. Arrange the apple slices on top of the pastry in the pan. In another bowl, mix the cinnamon, cloves and brown sugar. Sprinkle over the apples. Drain the raisins, discarding the rum. Distribute evenly over the apples.

To assemble, roll out the remaining pastry and place on top of the tart. Seal and flute the edges. Cut vents on top with a knife. Brush with the egg white mixture. Bake, uncovered, on the middle oven rack for approximately 35 to 40 minutes or until the crust is golden brown. Serve warm.

Prep Time: 35 minutes
Cook Time: 35-40 minutes

Nutritional Analysis
per serving

Calories	*471*
Fat	*5 g*
Sodium	*13 mg*
Protein	*6 g*
Carbohydrates	*91 g*
Cholesterol	*0 mg*

COCOA MINT BROWNIES

(Makes 18/Serves 18)

Prep Time: 45 minutes
Cook Time: 30-35 minutes

Nutritional Analysis
per serving

Calories	159
Fat	2 g
Sodium	42 mg
Protein	4 g
Carbohydrates	35 g
Cholesterol	less than 1 mg

Brownies:

	non-stick cooking spray
¾	cup cocoa powder
1	cup sugar
1	cup all-purpose flour
1	teaspoon baking powder
1	teaspoon vanilla extract
½	cup skim milk
3	egg whites
1	tablespoon olive oil

Preheat oven to 350°. Coat a 9-inch square baking dish with the cooking spray. In a large bowl, mix the cocoa powder, sugar, flour and baking powder. In a small bowl, mix the vanilla, milk and egg whites. Combine the dry and liquid ingredients in the larger bowl. Blend in the olive oil. Pour into the prepared dish. Bake, uncovered, on the center oven rack for approximately 30 to 35 minutes or until the edges pull from the sides of the dish. Do not overbake, the brownies should be moist in the center. Cool.

Frosting:

2½	cups confectioners' sugar
1	cup cocoa powder
½	cup skim milk
1½	teaspoons mint-flavored extract

In a bowl, mix the confectioners' sugar and cocoa powder. Gradually add the skim milk, beating constantly with an electric mixer until creamy. Add the mint extract. Blend thoroughly. To serve, spread the frosting with a rubber spatula over the cooled brownies.

It's easier to cut the brownies after they have been refrigerated. A sharp knife dipped in hot water and dried makes for a neater cut.

ALL AMERICAN

PEACH RUM COBBLER

(Serves 12)

Filling:

1	cup dark raisins
½	cup dark rum
¾	cup sugar
1	tablespoon cornstarch
5	cups sliced, peeled, fresh peaches

In a bowl, soak the raisins in the rum for 1 hour. Drain, reserving the rum. In a saucepan, combine the sugar and cornstarch. Add the reserved rum. Cook over medium heat, stirring constantly, for approximately 5 minutes or until the mixture is thick and bubbly. Add the raisins and peaches. Cook for 5 minutes longer. Pour the filling into a 1½-quart baking dish. Set aside to make the topping.

Topping:

1½	cups all-purpose flour
2	tablespoons sugar
1½	teaspoons baking powder
2	egg whites
½	cup skim milk

Preheat oven to 375°. In a bowl, combine the flour, sugar and baking powder. In another bowl, beat the egg whites and milk. Add to the dry ingredients. Stir until moistened.

To assemble, spread the topping over the hot filling. Bake, uncovered, for approximately 25 minutes or until golden brown.

This cobbler may be enjoyed à la mode by placing a scoop of lowfat frozen vanilla yogurt on top of each serving.

Prep Time: 30 minutes
Cook Time: 35 minutes
Misc Time: Soak raisins 1 hour

Nutritional Analysis
per serving

Calories	*210*
Fat	*less than 1 g*
Sodium	*69 mg*
Protein	*3 g*
Carbohydrates	*42 g*
Cholesterol	*less than 1 mg*

ALL AMERICAN

PUMPKIN CHEESECAKE
(Serves 12)

Prep Time: 25 minutes
Cook Time: 55 minutes
Misc Time: Chill 10 hours
to overnight

Nutritional Analysis
per serving

Calories	*135*
Fat	*less than 1 g*
Sodium	*83 mg*
Protein	*5 g*
Carbohydrates	*28 g*
Cholesterol	*0 mg*

	non-stick cooking spray
1	cup nonfat ricotta cheese
16	ounces nonfat cream cheese, softened
1	cup packed light brown sugar
¼	cup all-purpose flour
2	teaspoons ground cinnamon
¾	teaspoon ground ginger
¾	teaspoon ground nutmeg
½	teaspoon ground cloves
5	egg whites
1	16-ounce can pumpkin
½	teaspoon cream of tartar
⅓	cup sugar

Preheat oven to 350°. Lightly coat the bottom of a 9-inch springform pan with the cooking spray. Wrap the outside, bottom and sides with foil. Set aside. In a bowl or food processor, blend the ricotta cheese and cream cheese until smooth. Add the brown sugar, flour, cinnamon, ginger, nutmeg, cloves and 2 of the egg whites. Mix until smooth. Pour into a large bowl. Stir in the pumpkin. Set aside. In a bowl, beat the remaining 3 egg whites and cream of tartar at high speed with an electric mixer. Gradually add the sugar and beat until stiff peaks form. Gently fold into the pumpkin mixture. Spoon into the prepared springform pan. Place the springform pan into a larger, shallow pan. Add hot water to the larger pan to a depth of 1 inch. Bake, uncovered, for approximately 55 minutes or until set. Remove from the oven and take the springform pan out of the water pan. Cool. Remove the foil. Cover the top again with fresh foil. Chill, covered, for 10 hours to overnight. To serve, remove the side of the springform pan and place the cheesecake on a plate.

USA SOUTHERN

rowing up in Atlanta, Georgia, I had the opportunity to experience *Southern Hospitality* and cooking first hand. I can remember the Sunday dinner table covered with family favorites — fried chicken, mashed potatoes and gravy, fried vegetables and strawberry shortcake covered with whipped cream. The homemade biscuits were perfect for soaking up the chicken gravy made from pan drippings. It seemed so wonderful at the time. Little did I know that this food was loaded with fat and cholesterol, nor did I care. It was the way everyone enjoyed Sunday dinner. Even weekday meals were no different — ham, sausage and fried eggs for breakfast and pot roast, meatloaf and string beans cooked in bacon fat for supper. It all sounds so heavy to me now.

Despite its foibles in terms of cuisine, *Southern Hospitality* is the warmest and friendliest in the world. The preparation of food, however, can certainly be made lighter and healthier without losing any of its original flavor and tradition. Southern cooking is not only representative of the Deep South, but also encompasses a melting pot of international cuisines — African, Spanish and French. Each region has speciality dishes with their own particular flair, yet all are American.

Louisiana boasts two of the South's most popular cooking styles — Cajun and Creole. Cajun is native to the swamps and bayous while Creole is centered in New Orleans. To a great extent, both mimic classic French cuisine where spices, peppers, rice and seafood are considered staples.

After two years in New Orleans, I was off to Florida, another interesting state for cuisine. You might logically think that because Florida is located in the Southern section of the Untied States, it should be considered Southern. Well it *is* Southern, but not in the way that Georgia and Louisiana are. It's different — mainly because Florida is more or less one big peninsula inhabited by people (and cuisines) from all over the world. And, because it's surrounded by so much water, there are countless restaurants which all claim to have the best seafood in town. Fifteen years of living in Florida have taught me a thing or two. And now, it's my pleasure to teach you a few shortcuts to healthier Southern cooking.

USA SOUTHERN

BEER AND POTATO SOUP

(Serves 8)

Prep Time: 25 minutes
Cook Time: 35-40 minutes

Nutritional Analysis
per serving

Calories	144
Fat	3 g
Sodium	213 mg
Protein	6 g
Carbohydrates	20 g
Cholesterol	6 mg

2½	cups diced white potatoes
3	cups defatted chicken stock
½	cup finely chopped onion
1	tablespoon olive oil
2	tablespoons all-purpose flour
1	cup nonfat grated Parmesan cheese
2	cups lowfat milk
1	cup light beer
½	teaspoon hot pepper sauce
½	teaspoon white pepper
	parsley sprigs for garnish

In a stockpot, combine the potatoes, chicken stock and onion. Bring to a boil. Reduce heat to medium and cook, partially covered, for approximately 20 minutes or until the potatoes are tender. Drain, reserving 2 cups of the cooking liquid. In a large bowl, combine the potatoes and reserved cooking liquid. Heat the olive oil in the same stockpot. Stir in the flour and add the potato mixture. Mix in the Parmesan cheese. Add the milk, beer and hot pepper sauce. Cook until very hot, but do not boil. Add the white pepper. Garnish with parsley sprigs.

For even better flavor, make this soup a day ahead of time and store it in the refrigerator.

BRUNSWICK STEW

(Serves 8)

3½	pounds chicken breasts, skinned, cut into halves
½	cup all-purpose flour
2	tablespoons olive oil
4	medium onions, finely chopped
1½	quarts water
4	cups coarsely chopped, seeded tomatoes
¼	cup tomato paste
¼	cup lima beans (fresh or frozen)
¼	cup corn (fresh or frozen)
2	large red bell peppers, seeded, diced
4	large potatoes, peeled, cut into ½-inch cubes
1½	teaspoons cayenne pepper
2	teaspoons worcestershire sauce
1½	cups wine (red or white)

Prep Time: 50 minutes
Cook Time: 1¾ hours

Nutritional Analysis
per serving

Calories	341
Fat	6 g
Sodium	95 mg
Protein	32 g
Carbohydrates	30 g
Cholesterol	73 mg

In a bowl, dredge the chicken pieces in flour on both sides. In a large stockpot, cook the chicken in the olive oil over medium heat for approximately 10 minutes or until browned. Remove to a platter and set aside. In the same pot, brown the onion until soft and golden. Pour in the water. Add the chicken, tomato and tomato paste. Bring to a boil. Reduce heat and simmer, partially covered, for 1 hour. Stir occasionally. Add the lima beans, corn, red pepper, potatoes, cayenne pepper, worcestershire sauce and wine. Cook for approximately 30 minutes longer or until the vegetables are tender.

Brunswick Stew should be fairly thick. If it's too thin, remove the chicken and vegetables and reduce the liquid (but don't forget to replace them!) If it needs to be thinned out a bit, just add water.

OVEN "FRIED" CHICKEN

(Serves 6)

	non-stick cooking spray
3	cups plain bread crumbs
1	teaspoon salt
1	teaspoon white pepper
2	egg whites
¼	cup water
9	large chicken breasts, skinned, cut into halves

Preheat oven to 375°. Coat a shallow baking pan with the cooking spray. In a plastic food storage bag, mix the bread crumbs, salt and pepper. In a bowl, mix the egg whites and water. Dip the chicken pieces in the egg white mixture, coating thoroughly. Place the chicken in the bag and shake vigorously to cover with the bread crumb mixture. Place on the baking pan and coat the pieces lightly with the cooking spray. "Fry" on the middle oven rack for approximately 35 to 40 minutes or until tender and crispy, turning occasionally.

Now you can have all the benefits of traditional "fried" chicken the healthy way.

Prep Time: 20 minutes
Cook Time: 35-40 minutes

Nutritional Analysis
per serving

Calories	*417*
Fat	*6 g*
Sodium	*657 mg*
Protein	*51 g*
Carbohydrates	*37 g*
Cholesterol	*112 mg*

STUFFED CORNISH HENS

(Serves 8)

Hens:

	non-stick cooking spray
4	Cornish game hens

Preheat oven to 350°. Lightly coat a baking pan with the cooking spray. Clean the hens and remove the organs.

Stuffing:

4	garlic cloves, minced
1	large onion, finely chopped
½	cup finely chopped celery
1	tablespoon olive oil
5	cups freshly ground bread crumbs
¾	cup finely chopped parsley
2	teaspoons crushed sage
½	teaspoon black pepper
2	cups defatted chicken stock
1	cup dry white wine

In a skillet, sauté the garlic, onion and celery in the olive oil until golden. Add the bread crumbs, parsley, sage, pepper and chicken stock. Mix well. Fill the cavities of the hens with the stuffing and tie the legs together with twine. Tuck under the wings. Place the hens in the prepared baking pan and cover loosely with foil. Bake for 40 minutes. Remove the foil and continue baking for approximately 20 minutes longer or until the hens are thoroughly cooked and golden brown. Baste often with the pan juices. Transfer the hens to a heated platter, cut into halves and keep warm by covering with foil. Place the baking pan over medium heat, add the wine and stir to deglaze the pan juices. Pour the mixture over the hens. Serve hot.

Prep Time: 40 minutes
Cook Time: 65-70 minutes

Nutritional Analysis
per serving

Calories	*397*
Fat	*11 g*
Sodium	*309 mg*
Protein	*47 g*
Carbohydrates	*19 g*
Cholesterol	*131 mg*

BLACKEYED PEAS WITH RICE
(Serves 8)

Prep Time: 30 minutes
Cook Time: 1½ hours
Misc Time: Soak overnight

Nutritional Analysis
per serving

Calories	*373*
Fat	*3 g*
Sodium	*405 mg*
Protein	*17 g*
Carbohydrates	*70 g*
Cholesterol	*9 mg*

1	pound dried blackeyed peas
½	pound smoked turkey, cubed
1	cup finely chopped onion
4	garlic cloves, minced
1	tablespoon olive oil
2	quarts water
2	bay leaves
1	teaspoon thyme
1	tablespoon black pepper
2½	cups long grain white rice
	chopped onion for garnish
	red wine vinegar for garnish

In a pot, add enough water to cover the peas. Soak overnight. Discard any that float to the top. Drain, rinse and set aside. In a large pot, sauté the turkey, onion and garlic in the olive oil over medium heat until the onion is golden. Add the peas, water, bay leaves and thyme. Bring to a boil. Reduce heat and simmer, partially covered, for approximately 1 to 1½ hours or until the peas are tender. Add more water as needed to prevent the peas from drying out. Discard the bay leaves. Season with pepper. In a pot, bring water to a boil. Add the rice. Reduce heat and simmer, partially covered, for approximately 20 minutes or until tender and the water has been absorbed. To serve, spoon 1 cup of warm rice into individual dishes and ladle the peas over top. Garnish with chopped onion and sprinkle lightly with wine vinegar.

Traditionally, this dish is made with ham hocks instead of turkey. The turkey gives the smoked taste without the fat of ham.

HERB YELLOW RICE

(Serves 6)

3	cups water
2	cups long grain white rice
1	teaspoon saffron
2	tablespoons marjoram
2	tablespoons thyme
¼	cup minced parsley
2	tablespoons minced chives

In a pot, bring the water to a boil. Add the rice and saffron. Reduce heat and simmer, partially covered, for approximately 20 minutes or until tender and the water has been absorbed. Stir occasionally. To serve, spoon the rice into a bowl. Toss with the marjoram, thyme, parsley and chives.

Prep Time: 15 minutes
Cook Time: 25 minutes

Nutritional Analysis
per serving

Calories	*161*
Fat	*0 g*
Sodium	*181 mg*
Protein	*3 g*
Carbohydrates	*36 g*
Cholesterol	*0 mg*

OVEN "FRIED" GREEN TOMATOES

(Serves 6)

	non-stick cooking spray
2	egg whites
¼	cup water
2½	cups plain bread crumbs
¼	teaspoon black pepper
6	green tomatoes, thickly sliced

Preheat oven to 400°. Coat 2 baking sheets with the cooking spray. In a bowl, beat the egg whites and water. In another bowl, combine the bread crumbs and black pepper. Dip the tomato slices in the egg whites first and then dredge in the bread crumb mixture. Place the breaded tomato slices on the baking sheets and coat lightly with the cooking spray. Bake for approximately 25 to 30 minutes or until tender, crisp and slightly browned. Turn occasionally to prevent them from drying out.

This is a real Southern treat — one of my favorites.

Prep Time: 15 minutes
Cook Time: 25-30 minutes

Nutritional Analysis
per serving

Calories	*201*
Fat	*2 g*
Sodium	*339 mg*
Protein	*8 g*
Carbohydrates	*37 g*
Cholesterol	*2 mg*

Squash and Onion Sauté
(Serves 6)

Prep Time: 10 minutes
Cook Time: 5-7 minutes

Nutritional Analysis
per serving

Calories	37
Fat	4 g
Sodium	6 mg
Protein	1 g
Carbohydrates	8 g
Cholesterol	0 mg

	non-stick cooking spray
4	cups thinly sliced yellow squash
1	cup thinly sliced onion
1	garlic clove, minced
½	cup finely chopped parsley
¼	teaspoon white pepper

Coat a large skillet with the cooking spray. Add the squash, onion and garlic. Sauté over medium heat for approximately 5 to 7 minutes or until browned. Add the parsley. Mix well. Season with the pepper. Serve hot.

This is a wonderful vegetable dish to serve with Oven "Fried" Chicken (see page 146).

Southern Biscuits
(Makes 12/Serves 12)

Prep Time: 15 minutes
Cook Time: 10-12 minutes

Nutritional Analysis
per serving

Calories	141
Fat	4 g
Sodium	385 mg
Protein	4 g
Carbohydrates	23 g
Cholesterol	1 mg

3	cups all-purpose flour
1	teaspoon salt
1	tablespoon baking powder
1	teaspoon baking soda
3	tablespoons solid vegetable shortening
1½	cups buttermilk
	non-stick cooking spray

Preheat oven to 350°. In a bowl, sift the flour, salt, baking powder and baking soda. Cut in the shortening until the mixture is coarse. Mix in enough buttermilk to form a soft dough. Turn out onto a floured surface, kneading until smooth. Roll out to a ¾-inch thickness. Cut with a 2-inch cookie cutter. Coat a baking sheet with the cooking spray and place biscuits 1 inch apart. Bake on the center oven rack for approximately 10 to 12 minutes or until slightly browned.

APPLE BROWN BETTY

(Serves 12)

Pastry:

2	cups all-purpose flour
¼	cup sugar
2	teaspoons baking powder
¼	cup egg product
½	cup lowfat milk
	non-stick cooking spray

Preheat oven to 350°. In a bowl, mix the flour, sugar and baking powder. Stir in the egg product and milk. Coat a 9 x 9-inch baking dish with the cooking spray. Spread the mixture over the bottom of the dish. Set aside.

Filling:

1	cup packed dark brown sugar
2	tablespoons cornstarch
¼	teaspoon ground ginger
1½	cups water
½	cup raisins
8	cups sliced, peeled apples
1	tablespoon lemon juice
2	tablespoons sugar

In a saucepan, combine the brown sugar, cornstarch and ginger. Stir in the water and raisins. Cook over medium heat, stirring frequently, for approximately 5 minutes or until thickened and bubbly. Stir in the apples and lemon juice. Cook for approximately 5 minutes longer or until the apples are hot.

To assemble, pour the filling evenly over the dough in the baking dish. Sprinkle the top with 2 tablespoons of sugar. Bake, uncovered, for approximately 25 minutes or until the crust is brown on the bottom. Serve warm.

Prep Time: 35 minutes
Cook Time: 35 minutes

Nutritional Analysis
per serving

Calories	*250*
Fat	*1 g*
Sodium	*87 mg*
Protein	*3 g*
Carbohydrates	*58 g*
Cholesterol	*less than 1 mg*

BANANA PUDDING

(Serves 6)

Prep Time: 25 minutes
Cook Time: 10-15 minutes

Nutritional Analysis
per serving

Calories	347
Fat	5 g
Sodium	184 mg
Protein	9 g
Carbohydrates	66 g
Cholesterol	18 mg

Pudding:

½	cup sugar
2	tablespoons cornstarch
2	cups lowfat milk
½	cup egg product
1	teaspoon vanilla extract
1	teaspoon banana extract
36	lowfat vanilla wafers
6	large bananas, peeled, sliced

In a saucepan, combine the sugar and cornstarch. Add the milk. Cook over medium heat, stirring constantly, for approximately 5 minutes or until thickened and bubbly. Cook for 2 minutes longer. Remove from heat. Pour the egg product into a bowl. Gradually stir 1 cup of the hot mixture into the egg product. Return to the saucepan. Bring to a boil. Cook for 2 minutes longer, stirring constantly. Remove from heat. Stir in the vanilla and banana extracts.

Topping:

3	egg whites
2	tablespoons confectioners' sugar

In a bowl, beat the egg whites until stiff peaks form. Gradually add the confectioners' sugar, beating constantly until stiff.

To assemble, line the bottom of a 1½-quart oven-proof serving dish with vanilla wafers. Alternate layers of 1 cup pudding, sliced bananas and remaining vanilla wafers until all ingredients are used. Spread the topping lightly over the pudding to make decorative peaks, sealing all the edges. Preheat the broiler. Broil until the topping begins to turn golden brown. Serve chilled or at room temperature.

USA SOUTHERN

KEY LIME PIE
(Serves 8)

Crust:

3	cups graham cracker crumbs
3	tablespoons solid vegetable shortening
¾	cup sugar

Preheat oven to 400°. In a bowl, combine all ingredients. Blend well. Press the crust mixture into a 9-inch pie plate. Bake, uncovered, for approximately 12 minutes or until slightly browned. Remove from the oven and set aside.

Filling:

1	cup sugar
1	envelope unflavored gelatin
½	cup lime juice
½	cup water
¾	cup egg product
½	teaspoon finely shredded lime peel
3	egg whites
	lime slices for garnish
	nonfat whipped topping

In a saucepan, combine ⅔ cup sugar and gelatin. Mix in the lime juice, water and egg product. Cook, stirring constantly, over low heat for approximately 5 minutes or until the mixture thickens slightly. Remove from heat. Stir in the lime peel. Chill, uncovered, for approximately 30 minutes, stirring occasionally. Remove when the mixture has the consistency of syrup. In a separate bowl, beat the egg whites until soft peaks form. Gradually add the remaining ⅓ cup sugar, beating until stiff peaks form. Gently fold the beaten egg whites into the lime-gelatin mixture.

To assemble, pour the filling into the baked crust and smooth with a spatula. Chill, uncovered, for 4 hours or until set. Garnish with the lime slices and whipped topping.

Prep Time: 40 minutes
Cook Time: 15-20 minutes
Misc Time: Chill 4½ hours

Nutritional Analysis
per serving

Calories	*409*
Fat	*9 g*
Sodium	*319 mg*
Protein	*7 g*
Carbohydrates	*75 g*
Cholesterol	*0 mg*

USA SOUTHERN

STRAWBERRY SHORTCAKE
(Serves 8)

Prep Time: 35 minutes
Cook Time: 15-20 minutes

Nutritional Analysis
per serving

Calories	*292*
Fat	*3 g*
Sodium	*269 mg*
Protein	*6 g*
Carbohydrates	*56 g*
Cholesterol	*less than 1 mg*

Shortcake:

3	cups all-purpose flour
1½	tablespoons baking powder
¼	cup sugar
4	ounces nonfat cream cheese, softened
¼	cup egg product
¾	cup skim milk
1	egg white
1	tablespoon water

Preheat oven to 375°. In a bowl, sift the flour, baking powder and sugar. Blend in the cream cheese. Mix in the egg product and enough milk to form a firm dough. Knead lightly on a floured surface and roll out to ¾-inch thickness. Using a 3-inch circle cutter, cut into an even number of pieces. In another bowl, beat the egg white and water. Place 1 circle on top of another, pressing down slightly. Brush the top piece with the egg white mixture. Place on a baking sheet. Bake, uncovered, on the middle oven rack for 15 to 20 minutes or until slightly browned. Cool before transferring to a wire rack.

Filling:

1½	pounds fresh strawberries, hulled
2	tablespoons confectioners' sugar
5	tablespoons liqueur (orange or strawberry)
2	cups nonfat whipped topping
	confectioners' sugar for decorative topping

In a food processor, combine ½ of the strawberries, 2 tablespoons confectioners' sugar and liqueur. Purée for 10 to 15 seconds. Cut the remaining strawberries into halves and mix with the purée.

To assemble, separate the shortcakes into halves and place the bottoms on serving plates. Spoon the filling over the bottoms and add the whipped topping. Place the remaining half of the shortcake on top. Dust lightly with the confectioners' sugar. Serve cold.

SWEET POTATO PIE

(Serves 8)

Pastry:

2	cups all-purpose flour
2	tablespoons solid vegetable shortening
1	tablespoon sugar
1	teaspoon ground cinnamon
	ice water

Prep Time: 45 minutes
Cook Time: 1 hour 20 minutes

Nutritional Analysis
per serving

Calories	*316*
Fat	*4 g*
Sodium	*57 mg*
Protein	*7 g*
Carbohydrates	*63 g*
Cholesterol	*3 mg*

Preheat oven to 375°. In a bowl, mix the flour, shortening, sugar and cinnamon with a fork or pastry cutter until coarse. Gradually add enough ice water to form a soft dough. Roll out onto a floured board to ¼-inch thickness to fit a 9-inch pie plate. Place the dough in the pie plate and flute the edge decoratively.

Filling:

3	large sweet potatoes
3	egg whites
¾	cup sugar
2	teaspoons cinnamon
1	teaspoon nutmeg
1	teaspoon ground cloves
2	cups lowfat milk

Peel the potatoes and cut into small pieces. In a large pot, bring water to a boil. Add the potatoes. Cook, partially covered, for approximately 20 minutes or until tender. Drain. Cool for 10 minutes. In a large bowl, combine the potatoes with the remaining ingredients. Beat with an electric mixer or by hand with a wire whisk until well blended.

To assemble, pour the sweet potato mixture into the prepared pie plate. Bake, uncovered, for approximately 1 hour or until set. Serve warm or at room temperature.

CRAWFISH BISQUE

(Serves 8)

Prep Time: 45 minutes
Cook Time: 3 hours

*Nutritional Analysis
per serving*

Calories	442
Fat	6 g
Sodium	912 mg
Protein	20 g
Carbohydrates	66 g
Cholesterol	36 mg

Crawfish:

32	crawfish

Separate the crawfish heads and tails. Clean the heads by removing the guts and rinsing thoroughly. Remove the meat from the tails and set aside.

Stuffing:

3	large onions, peeled, quartered
3	green bell peppers, seeded, cut into large pieces
8	celery stalks, trimmed, cut into large pieces
10	garlic cloves, peeled
2	cups parsley sprigs
10	green onion stalks, trimmed, cut into large pieces
½	cup fresh oregano
½	cup fresh basil
4	cups plain bread crumbs
12	egg whites
1	cup worcestershire sauce
2	teaspoons hot pepper sauce

In a food processor, blend the onion, green pepper, celery, garlic, parsley, green onion, oregano and basil alternately with the crawfish meat until all ingredients have been ground. This may take several times in the processor depending on the size of the bowl. In a large bowl, combine the ground ingredients, bread crumbs, egg whites, worcestershire sauce and hot pepper sauce. Blend well. Stuff the mixture into the cleaned crawfish heads. Chill the stuffed heads while making the gravy for the bisque.

For pre-cooked fresh or frozen crawfish, remember that your cooking time will decrease (see Fundamentals page 10).

continued on next page

CRAWFISH BISQUE (CONTINUED)

Gravy:

2	tablespoons olive oil
½	cup all-purpose flour
½	cup finely chopped onion
½	cup finely chopped green bell pepper
½	cup finely chopped celery
4	garlic cloves, minced
½	cup finely chopped parsley
4	cups finely chopped, seeded, peeled tomatoes
¼	cup worcestershire sauce
2	teaspoons hot pepper sauce
2	quarts water
4	bay leaves
½	cup white wine

In a saucepan, make a roux with the olive oil and flour, stirring constantly, until the color is a deep brown. Add the onion, green pepper, celery, garlic, parsley, tomato, worcestershire sauce, hot pepper sauce and water. Add the bay leaves and wine. Simmer, partially covered, for approximately 2 hours. Add the stuffed crawfish heads. Simmer for 1 hour longer to enhance all flavors. Discard the bay leaves. To serve, place 4 crawfish heads into individual serving bowls and ladle the gravy over top.

New Orleans favorite, Crawfish Bisque, is usually made with bacon drippings and other saturated fats. This is a much lighter and more delicious version.

USA SOUTHERN

SEAFOOD GUMBO
(Serves 8)

Prep Time: 25 minutes
Cook Time: 1³/4 hours

Nutritional Analysis
per serving

Calories	*328*
Fat	*5 g*
Sodium	*794 mg*
Protein	*34 g*
Carbohydrates	*34 g*
Cholesterol	*145 mg*

1	pound medium shrimp
2	tablespoons olive oil
¹/₃	cup all-purpose flour
1	cup finely chopped onion
4	garlic cloves, minced
3	cups coarsely chopped, seeded, peeled tomatoes
¹/₂	cup white wine
1¹/₂	pounds fresh okra, stems removed
2	quarts water
2	teaspoons salt
1	teaspoon crushed red pepper
2	large bay leaves
¹/₂	teaspoon thyme
¹/₂	teaspoon allspice
¹/₂	pound grouper or red snapper filet, cut into small cubes
¹/₂	pound sea scallops
¹/₂	cup finely chopped green onion
1	cup finely chopped parsley
1¹/₃	cups long grain white rice

Peel and devein the shrimp, removing the shells completely. Set aside. In a stockpot, warm the olive oil over medium heat. Stir in the flour to make a roux. Add the onion and garlic. Sauté until the onion is soft. Add the tomato and wine. Cook, uncovered, over low heat for 20 minutes, stirring frequently. Mix in the okra. Cook for 10 minutes longer. Add the water, salt, red pepper and bay leaves. Cook, partially covered, for 30 minutes. Add the thyme, allspice and seafood. Cook for approximately 15 minutes longer or until the seafood is tender. Remove from heat. Stir in the green onion and parsley. Discard the bay leaves. In a pot, bring water to a boil. Add the rice. Reduce heat and simmer, partially covered, for approximately 20 minutes or until tender and the water has been absorbed. To serve, spoon ¹/₂ cup of rice into individual bowls and ladle the gumbo over top.

USA SOUTHERN

CRAWFISH ÉTOUFFÉE

(Serves 6)

2	pounds crawfish
2	large onions, finely chopped
2	celery stalks, finely chopped
3	garlic cloves, minced
1	medium green bell pepper, finely chopped
2	tablespoons olive oil
2	teaspoons hot pepper sauce
3	tablespoons all-purpose flour
4	cups defatted chicken stock
2	scallions, coarsely chopped
1	tablespoon coarsely chopped parsley
½	teaspoon black pepper

Prep Time: 25 minutes
Cook Time: 40 minutes

Nutritional Analysis
per serving

Calories	*187*
Fat	*6 g*
Sodium	*221 mg*
Protein	*15 g*
Carbohydrates	*16 g*
Cholesterol	*94 mg*

Remove the meat from the crawfish tails and set aside. Discard the shells. In a large skillet, sauté the onion, celery, garlic and green pepper in the olive oil over low heat for 25 minutes. Add the hot pepper sauce and crawfish meat. Sauté for 1 minute longer. Stir in the flour. Cook for 2 minutes longer. Add the chicken stock, scallions, parsley and black pepper. Simmer, partially covered, for approximately 15 minutes or until very hot.

Serve with white rice for a more complete meal. Also, don't forget to reduce your cooking time if using pre-cooked fresh or frozen crawfish (see Fundamentals page 10).

BLACKENED RED SNAPPER
(Serves 8)

Prep Time: 15 minutes
Cook Time: 15 minutes

Nutritional Analysis
per serving

Calories	154
Fat	2 g
Sodium	65 mg
Protein	32 g
Carbohydrates	2 g
Cholesterol	53 mg

8	4-ounce red snapper filets
	non-stick cooking spray
1	teaspoon garlic powder
2	teaspoons onion powder
2	teaspoons white pepper
2	teaspoons black pepper
1	teaspoon cayenne pepper
2	teaspoons crushed oregano
2	teaspoons crushed parsley
	lemon slices for garnish

Coat both sides of the snapper filets lightly with the cooking spray. In a shallow bowl, mix the garlic powder, onion powder, white pepper, black pepper, cayenne pepper, crushed oregano and crushed parsley. Dredge the snapper filets in the seasoning on both sides. In a very hot skillet, sear the filets for approximately 7 minutes per side or until well crusted. Garnish with lemon slices. Serve immediately.

And you thought only fancy restaurants could blacken fish properly...

USA Southern

CRAWFISH PASTA
(Serves 6)

Sauce:

24	crawfish
1	large green bell pepper, seeded, thinly sliced
1	large onion, thinly sliced
4	garlic cloves, minced
½	cup thinly sliced okra
2	tablespoons olive oil
1	teaspoon crushed red pepper
2	large tomatoes, peeled, seeded, coarsely chopped
½	teaspoon thyme
1	teaspoon salt
1	cup dry white wine

Remove the meat from the crawfish tails and cut into small pieces. Discard the shells. In a skillet, sauté the green pepper, onion, garlic and okra in the olive oil. Add the red pepper, tomato, thyme, salt and wine. Cook, uncovered, over medium heat for 15 minutes. Add the crawfish meat. Cook for 5 minutes longer.

Pasta:

1	pound pasta (angel hair, linguine or spaghetti)
1	cup finely chopped parsley

In a large pot, cook the pasta until *al dente*. Drain. Serve on individual plates and ladle the crawfish sauce over top. Sprinkle with the freshly chopped parsley.

Crawfish Pasta is a delicious variation of standard Creole cuisine. Actually, it brings out the best in two of my favorites, Creole and Italian. Remember to reduce the cooking time if you're using pre-cooked crawfish (see Fundamentals page 10).

Prep Time: 25 minutes
Cook Time: 35-40 minutes

Nutritional Analysis
per serving

Calories	394
Fat	5 g
Sodium	390 mg
Protein	15 g
Carbohydrates	64 g
Cholesterol	30 mg

SHRIMP JAMBALAYA

(Serves 6)

Shrimp Jambalaya
Prep Time: 30 minutes
Cook Time: 1 hour

Nutritional Analysis
per serving

Calories	*418*
Fat	*5 g*
Sodium	*178 mg*
Protein	*13 g*
Carbohydrates	*74 g*
Cholesterol	*65 mg*

Shrimp and Chicken Jambalaya
Prep Time: 40 minutes
Cook Time: 1½ hours

Nutritional Analysis
per serving

Calories	*469*
Fat	*6 g*
Sodium	*181 mg*
Protein	*23 g*
Carbohydrates	*73 g*
Cholesterol	*75 mg*

24	large shrimp
1	large onion, finely chopped
1	large green bell pepper, finely chopped
4	garlic cloves, minced
2	tablespoons olive oil
3	cups long grain white rice
4	cups water
1	cup white wine
2	cups coarsely chopped, seeded, peeled tomatoes
1	teaspoon thyme
2	bay leaves
½	cup finely chopped parsley
2	teaspoons hot pepper sauce
	chopped parsley for garnish

Peel and devein the shrimp, removing the shells completely. In a large skillet, sauté the onion, green pepper and garlic in the olive oil until the onion is soft. Add the rice, water, wine, tomato, thyme and bay leaves. Bring to a boil. Reduce heat and simmer, partially covered, for 35 minutes. Add the shrimp, parsley and hot pepper sauce. Cook for approximately 15 minutes longer or until the liquid has been absorbed. Discard the bay leaves. To serve, spoon onto individual plates. Garnish with freshly chopped parsley.

For variety, use ½ pound of boneless, skinless chicken breast pieces along with the shrimp if more meat is desired.

USA SOUTHERN

RED BEANS AND RICE

(Serves 10)

2	pounds dried kidney beans
½	pound smoked turkey, cut into large pieces
12	cups water
½	teaspoon salt
2	teaspoons hot pepper sauce
2	teaspoons worcestershire sauce
1	cup finely chopped onion
2	bay leaves
3⅓	cups long grain white rice
	chopped onion for garnish
	red wine vinegar for garnish

Prep Time: 20 minutes
Cook Time: 2-2½ hours
Misc Time: Soak overnight

Nutritional Analysis
per serving

Calories	*463*
Fat	*1 g*
Sodium	*492 mg*
Protein	*22 g*
Carbohydrates	*90 g*
Cholesterol	*8 mg*

In a pot, add enough water to cover the beans. Soak overnight. Discard any that float to the top. Drain. In a large pot, combine the beans, turkey, water, salt, hot pepper sauce, worcestershire sauce, onion and bay leaves. Bring to a boil, stirring frequently. Reduce heat and simmer, partially covered, for approximately 1½ to 2 hours or until tender. Stir occasionally. Add more water if the beans are drying out. Remove 2 cups of the beans, mash and return to the pot. Cook for 30 minutes longer. In another pot, bring water to a boil. Add the rice. Reduce heat and simmer, partially covered, for approximately 20 minutes or until tender and the water has been absorbed. To serve, place 1 cup of rice onto individual plates and ladle the beans over top. Garnish with chopped onion and sprinkle with wine vinegar.

Red Beans and Rice is the epitome of New Orleans cuisine. The version to which I was first introduced contained ham and sausage. Instead, the smoked turkey in my recipe produces the taste of ham without all the fat.

BREAD PUDDING

(Serves 6)

Prep Time: 20 minutes
Cook Time: 40 minutes

Nutritional Analysis
per serving

Calories	*246*
Fat	*2 g*
Sodium	*146 mg*
Protein	*6 g*
Carbohydrates	*42 g*
Cholesterol	*3 mg*

Pudding:

¾	cup egg product
2	cups lowfat milk
⅓	cup sugar
½	teaspoon ground cinnamon
1	teaspoon vanilla extract
2½	cups dry bread cubes
⅓	cup raisins

Preheat oven to 325°. In a bowl, beat the egg product, milk, sugar, cinnamon and vanilla. Set aside. Place the bread cubes in a 9-inch baking dish and sprinkle with raisins. Pour the milk mixture over top. Bake on the center oven rack for approximately 40 minutes or until a knife inserted in the center comes out clean. Cool slightly while making the sauce.

Whiskey Sauce:

½	cup sugar
¼	cup water
1	teaspoon margarine
2	jiggers bourbon whiskey

In a saucepan, cook the sugar, water and margarine over medium heat until the sugar has dissolved. Stir in the whiskey. To serve, spoon equal amounts of the pudding into individual dishes and cover with the sauce. Serve warm.

Facing page — USA Southwest (pictured clockwise): Ginger Lime Sorbet, Flour Tortillas, Pepper Corn Relish, Swordfish with Melon Salsa, Spicy Southwestern Rice, Chicken Fajitas

USA SOUTHWEST

Beverage Suggestions

WINE

Wine Spritzers
with Club Soda, Chablis, Chardonnay or Blush
Fruit Garnish

Margaritas

Tequila Daiquiris with Fruit Flavors
Banana, Peach, Strawberry

Red or White Sangria with Fruit Garnish
Lemon, Orange, Pineapple

BEER

Poultry/Seafood	• Pilsner
Pasta	• Pilsner
Vegetables	• Pilsner
Chili/Rice/Refried Beans	• Pilsner • Mild Ale
Desserts	• Lambic • Weisse

COFFEE

Start with Colombian Coffee
and add the flavors of your choice:
Sugar and Cinnamon
Tia Maria
Kahlúa

USA SOUTHWEST

The Southwestern region of the United States is a contrast of climate and topography — from the cool mountains to hot deserts to warm Gulf Beaches. Most of the influence in Southwestern cooking comes from the Native Americans and Hispanics — which makes for a very interesting combination. Corn, beans and chili peppers (just to name a few) are ingredients used often, but in various ways. Southwestern cooking allows you to be creative — it's appeal is in its uniqueness. Unlike the French and Italian cuisines which have deep historical roots, there really are no rules here. Any fresh fruits and vegetables can be used to make wonderful salsas. And it's these salsas that make the cuisine not only delicious, but colorful and festive.

I've visited many restaurants in the western United States and sampled some of the most innovative meals. But truly, half the intrigue for me was in the presentation — the food was served on colorfully glazed terra-cotta dishes, garnishes were wildly creative and even the atmosphere made the food taste better.

Perhaps today, the most popular Southwestern food is fajitas. They are so much fun to both prepare *and* to serve. Not only are fajitas well balanced and delicious, but preparation time is quick, too. When I make them for my family and friends, I always feel as though I'm having a party, even if it's only the middle of the week.

This section will feature light versions of some of the best known Southwest dishes in addition to some creations of my own.

USA SOUTHWEST

SPICY VEGETARIAN CHILI

(Serves 10)

Prep Time: 1½ hours
Cook Time: 1¾ hours

Nutritional Analysis
per serving

Calories	*385*
Fat	*2 g*
Sodium	*596 mg*
Protein	*17 g*
Carbohydrates	*70 g*
Cholesterol	*0 mg*

1	pound dried kidney beans
1	pound dried pinto beans
3	garlic cloves, minced
2	cups thinly sliced onion
1	tablespoon olive oil
2	cups thinly sliced mushrooms
2	cups yellow corn
1	cup thinly sliced green bell pepper
2	28-ounce cans tomatoes, drained, peeled, coarsely chopped
	juice from canned tomatoes
1	green chili pepper, seeded, finely chopped
2	cups beer
3	tablespoons chili powder
1	tablespoon cumin
1	teaspoon salt

In a large pot, add enough water to cover the kidney beans and pinto beans. Cover and bring to a rapid boil. Remove from heat. Let stand for 1 hour. Simmer, partially covered, for 45 minutes, stirring occasionally. Drain, rinse and set aside. In a large pot, sauté the garlic and onion in the olive oil until golden. Stir in the beans, mushrooms, corn, green pepper, tomatoes, tomato juice and chili pepper. Bring to a boil. Add the beer, chili powder, cumin and salt. Reduce heat and simmer, partially covered, for approximately 45 minutes or until the beans are tender, stirring frequently. Serve hot.

USA Southwest

Mixed Bean Salad

(Serves 10)

2	cups green beans
1	cup dried black beans
1	cup dried pinto beans
1	cup dried kidney beans
½	cup coarsely chopped onion
½	cup coarsely chopped parsley
2	tablespoons olive oil
¼	cup red wine vinegar
1	teaspoon sugar
1	teaspoon salt
1	teaspoon black pepper

In a pot, blanch the green beans. Drain and set aside. In separate pots, add enough water to cover the black beans, pinto beans and kidney beans. Cover and bring to a rapid boil. Remove from heat. Let stand for 1 hour. Simmer, partially covered, for approximately 1 to 1½ hours or until tender, stirring occasionally. Drain, rinse and cool. In a large bowl, mix all beans and the remaining ingredients. Chill, covered, for 3 hours to overnight.

This dish may be prepared a day ahead of time and kept in the refrigerator until ready to serve.

Prep Time: 1½ hours
Cook Time: 1¼ -1¾ hours
Misc Time: Chill 3 hours
to overnight

Nutritional Analysis
per serving

Calories	*115*
Fat	*3 g*
Sodium	*242 mg*
Protein	*5 g*
Carbohydrates	*18 g*
Cholesterol	*0 mg*

USA SOUTHWEST

Prep Time: 25 minutes
Cook Time: 10-15 minutes
Misc Time: Chill 4 hours
           to overnight

Nutritional Analysis
per serving

Calories	495
Fat	12 g
Sodium	778 mg
Protein	46 g
Carbohydrates	45 g
Cholesterol	97 mg

CHICKEN FAJITAS

(Makes 12/Serves 6)

Fajita Marinade:

³/₄	cup worcestershire sauce
¹/₄	cup lime juice
1	teaspoon minced garlic
1	teaspoon finely chopped green onion
¹/₂	teaspoon salt
¹/₄	teaspoon crushed red pepper
1	tablespoon red wine vinegar

In a bowl, mix all ingredients. Chill, covered, for 4 hours to overnight.

Fajitas:

2	large onions
8	large chicken breast filets, skinned
2	tablespoons olive oil
	fajita marinade (see above)
12	Four Tortillas (see page 179)

Cut the onions into halves and slice into medium thick pieces. Thinly slice the longer sides of the chicken breasts. In a large skillet, cook the onion and chicken in the olive oil over high heat for approximately 6 to 8 minutes or until well browned. To serve, add the marinade to the chicken and onion mixture in the skillet. Heat for approximately 3 minutes or until sizzling. Serve immediately with warm tortillas.

SHRIMP FAJITAS
(Makes 12/Serves 6)

Fajita Marinade:

¾	cup worcestershire sauce
¼	cup lime juice
1	teaspoon minced garlic
1	teaspoon finely chopped green onion
½	teaspoon salt
¼	teaspoon crushed red pepper
1	tablespoon red wine vinegar

In a bowl, mix all ingredients. Chill, covered, for 4 hours to overnight.

Fajitas:

1	pound medium shrimp
2	large onions
2	tablespoons olive oil
	fajita marinade (see above)
12	Four Tortillas (see page 179)

Peel and devein the shrimp, removing the shells completely. Cut the onions into halves and slice into medium thick pieces. In a large skillet, cook the onion and shrimp in the olive oil over high heat for approximately 3 to 5 minutes or until the shrimp turn pink and slightly golden. To serve, add the marinade to the shrimp and onion mixture in the skillet. Heat for approximately 1 minute or until sizzling. Serve immediately with warm tortillas.

Prep Time: 25 minutes
Cook Time: 5-7 minutes
Misc Time: Chill 1 hours
to overnight

Nutritional Analysis
per serving

Calories	*318*
Fat	*9 g*
Sodium	*664 mg*
Protein	*11 g*
Carbohydrates	*45 g*
Cholesterol	*43 mg*

SWORDFISH WITH MELON SALSA

(Serves 6)

Prep Time: 35 minutes
Cook Time: 15-20 minutes
Misc Time: Marinate 2 hours

Nutritional Analysis
per serving

Calories	*217*
Fat	*5 g*
Sodium	*384 mg*
Protein	*30 g*
Carbohydrates	*7 g*
Cholesterol	*55 mg*

Marinade:

¾	cup worcestershire sauce
2	teaspoons finely chopped green onion
3	tablespoons lime juice
1	teaspoon minced garlic
½	small banana pepper, thinly sliced

In a small bowl, mix all ingredients. Set aside.

Swordfish:

6	5-ounce swordfish steaks

Place the fish in a shallow pan. Pour in the marinade. Marinate, covered, in the refrigerator for at least 2 hours. Preheat grill to a high flame. Remove the fish and discard the marinade. Grill over the high flame for approximately 15 to 20 minutes or until the fish is cooked through, but still tender.

Melon Salsa:

1	cup diced honeydew melon
½	cup finely chopped green onion
2	tablespoons finely chopped banana pepper
½	cup coarsely chopped, seeded tomatoes (green or yellow)
1	tablespoon sugar
1	tablespoon white wine vinegar

In a bowl, mix all ingredients. Refrigerate, covered, until ready for use. To serve, spoon the salsa over the grilled swordfish.

Use cantaloupe or other melons for different flavors and colors.

USA SOUTHWEST

TROUT WITH SWEET PEPPERS

(Serves 8)

	non-stick cooking spray
4	8-ounce whole trout
2	cups thinly sliced onion
2	large red bell peppers, seeded, thinly sliced
4	large garlic cloves, minced
1	cup white wine
1	teaspoon salt
1	cup finely chopped fresh parsley

Preheat oven to 350°. Coat a large baking dish with the cooking spray. Clean and gut the trout. Place in the prepared baking dish. Loosely separate the onion slices. Arrange the onion, peppers and garlic evenly over the fish. Pour in the wine. Sprinkle with the salt and parsley. Bake, uncovered, for approximately 25 to 30 minutes or until the fish is flaky. Baste with the pan juices every 5 minutes. Do not overcook. Transfer the fish to a heated serving platter. Remove the heads, tails and skin before serving. In a saucepan, combine the pan juices and vegetables. Warm until very hot. Spoon the vegetables and juices over the fish. Serve immediately.

Spicy Southwestern Rice (see page 177) is an excellent accompaniment to Trout with Sweet Peppers.

Prep Time: 20 minutes
Cook Time: 30-35 minutes

Nutritional Analysis
per serving

Calories	*179*
Fat	*3 g*
Sodium	*306 mg*
Protein	*26 g*
Carbohydrates	*5 g*
Cholesterol	*65 mg*

USA Southwest

Prep Time: 20 minutes
Cook Time: 30 minutes

Nutritional Analysis
per serving

Calories	551
Fat	11 g
Sodium	432 mg
Protein	16 g
Carbohydrates	91 g
Cholesterol	0 mg

Southwest Pasta

(Serves 4)

Sauce:

1	cup thinly sliced onion
4	garlic cloves, minced
1	cup thinly sliced red bell pepper
1	cup thinly sliced mushrooms
2	tablespoons olive oil
½	cup sliced black olives
1	cup coarsely chopped, seeded tomatoes
1	tablespoon chili powder
1	teaspoon crushed red pepper
½	cup finely chopped parsley
½	teaspoon salt
½	cup white wine

In a large skillet, sauté the onion, garlic, red bell pepper and mushrooms in the olive oil until the mushrooms are browned. Add the olives, tomato, chili powder, crushed red pepper, parsley and salt. Cook over high heat for 2 minutes. Pour in the wine. Cook for 1 minute longer.

Pasta:

1	pound pasta (angel hair, linguine or spaghetti)

In a large pot, cook the pasta until *al dente*. Drain. To serve, place the pasta in a bowl and mix in the sauce. Serve hot.

This dish combines 2 distinctly different cuisines — Italian and Southwestern. The result is a delicious variation of each.

CHILIED GREEN BEANS

(Serves 6)

	non-stick olive oil cooking spray
1	pound fresh green beans
1	teaspoon minced garlic
½	cup finely sliced green onion
2	teaspoons chili powder

Coat a large skillet with the cooking spray. Rinse, trim and dry the green beans. Sauté all ingredients over medium heat for approximately 20 minutes or until the beans are tender. Serve hot.

This is a simple and colorful recipe for green beans. The chili powder gives both color and a little life to this well-known vegetable.

Prep Time: 25 minutes
Cook Time: 20 minutes

*Nutritional Analysis
per serving*

Calories	*33*
Fat	*0 g*
Sodium	*11 mg*
Protein	*1 g*
Carbohydrates	*6 g*
Cholesterol	*0 mg*

USA Southwest

Refried Beans

(Serves 8)

Prep Time: 1¼ hours
Cook Time: 1½ hours

Nutritional Analysis
per serving

Calories   203
Fat   less than 1 g
Sodium   541 mg
Protein   16 g
Carbohydrates   32 g
Cholesterol   5 mg

1	pound dried pinto beans
2	bay leaves
	non-stick cooking spray
1	teaspoon hot pepper sauce
1	teaspoon salt
2	cups nonfat shredded Monterey Jack or Mozzarella cheese

In a pot, add enough water to cover the beans. Bring to a rapid boil. Remove from heat. Let stand for 1 hour. Add the bay leaves. Simmer, partially covered, for approximately 1 hour longer or until tender, stirring occasionally. Drain the beans, reserving 2 cups of the cooking liquid. Discard the bay leaves. Coat a large frying pan with the cooking spray. Add the beans and reserved cooking liquid. Cook over medium heat, mashing ⅔ of the beans with the back of a spoon until a medium-smooth consistency. Leave the remaining beans whole. Add the hot pepper sauce and salt. Spread the beans evenly in the pan. Cook, uncovered, over medium heat for approximately 15 minutes or until the bottom is firmly set but not browned. Flip the beans over. Cook for 5 minutes longer or until set. Top with the cheese and cook until it melts. Serve warm.

SPICY SOUTHWESTERN RICE

(Serves 6)

2	cups dried red kidney beans
4	cups water
2	cups long grain white rice
1	teaspoon minced garlic
1	cup finely chopped onion
2	tablespoons olive oil
2	teaspoons saffron
1	cup finely chopped parsley
2	tablespoons ground cumin
1	teaspoon crushed red pepper
½	teaspoon salt

Prep Time: 1½ hours
Cook Time: 1½-2 hours

Nutritional Analysis
per serving

Calories	*316*
Fat	*4 g*
Sodium	*191 mg*
Protein	*8 g*
Carbohydrates	*60 g*
Cholesterol	*0 mg*

In a pot, add enough water to cover the beans. Bring to a rapid boil. Remove from heat. Let stand for 1 hour. Simmer, partially covered, for approximately 1 hour longer or until tender, stirring occasionally. Drain, rinse and set aside. In a pot, bring the water to a boil. Add the rice. Reduce heat and simmer, partially covered, for approximately 20 minutes or until tender and the water has been absorbed. In a large skillet, sauté the garlic and onion in the olive oil until golden. Add the beans, rice, saffron, parsley, cumin, red pepper and salt. Mix well. Cook over medium heat, partially covered, for approximately 10 minutes or until well blended. Add more water as needed.

This is a delicious accompaniment to Chicken Fajitas (see page 170) and Shrimp Fajitas (see page 171).

USA SOUTHWEST

PEPPER CORN RELISH
(Serves 12)

Prep Time: 25 minutes
Cook Time: 20 minutes

Nutritional Analysis
per serving

Calories	40
Fat	0 g
Sodium	93 mg
Protein	1 g
Carbohydrates	9 g
Cholesterol	0 mg

2	cups frozen yellow corn, thawed
½	cup finely chopped banana peppers
½	cup finely chopped onion
½	cup finely chopped pimentos
½	cup white wine vinegar
2	tablespoons sugar
2	tablespoons water
½	teaspoon salt

In a small saucepan, combine all ingredients. Bring to a boil. Reduce heat and simmer, uncovered, for 20 minutes or until the corn is tender. Cool. Chill, covered, until ready for use.

Pepper Corn Relish is a welcome complement to any Southwestern entrée. You can prepare it a day ahead of time for enhanced flavor.

PICO DE GALLO
(Serves 8)

Prep Time: 20 minutes

Nutritional Analysis
per serving

Calories	10
Fat	0 g
Sodium	19 mg
Protein	less than 1 g
Carbohydrates	2 g
Cholesterol	0 mg

1	cup finely chopped, seeded tomatoes
½	cup finely chopped onion
½	cup finely chopped green bell pepper
½	teaspoon hot pepper sauce

In a small bowl, mix all ingredients. Chill, covered, until ready for use.

Pico de Gallo can be served with almost any Southwestern dish. Spoon it over Fajitas (see pages 170 and 171) for a spicy addition to the chicken or shrimp. It even offers a change of pace to everyday fish entrées.

USA SOUTHWEST

FLOUR TORTILLAS

(Makes 12/Serves 6)

4	cups all-purpose flour
1	tablespoon baking powder
½	teaspoon salt
2	tablespoons olive oil
1½	cups hot water
	non-stick cooking spray

In a bowl, sift the flour, baking powder and salt. Stir in the olive oil until the mixture is coarse. Add the water and mix until absorbed. Knead gently, adding more flour if the dough is too sticky. Let stand, covered with plastic wrap, for 20 minutes. Divide the dough into 12 equal portions. On a floured surface, roll into balls. Cover again. Let stand for 20 minutes longer. Roll each ball into an 8-inch circle on a floured surface. Keep the circles covered while rolling the remaining dough. Coat a skillet with the cooking spray and warm over high heat. Place the tortillas 1 at a time in the hot skillet. Cook until the tortillas start to bubble and are slightly browned. Flip over to cook the other side, pressing down lightly to flatten. After cooking, stack and set aside until ready for use.

Prep Time: 50 minutes
Cook Time: 30 minutes

*Nutritional Analysis
per serving*

Calories	*309*
Fat	*5 g*
Sodium	*391 mg*
Protein	*7 g*
Carbohydrates	*58 g*
Cholesterol	*0 mg*

USA SOUTHWEST

FROZEN MIXED BERRY MOLD
(Serves 10)

Prep Time: 35 minutes
Misc Time: Freeze overnight

Nutritional Analysis
per serving

Calories	*108*
Fat	*1 g*
Sodium	*21 mg*
Protein	*2 g*
Carbohydrates	*23 g*
Cholesterol	*0 mg*

	non-stick cooking spray
2	tablespoons lime juice
½	cup water
1	cup sugar
3	ounces blueberries
3	ounces raspberries
3	ounces boysenberries
3	ounces strawberries
5	tablespoons water
4	egg whites
1	cup nonfat whipped topping
	lime slices for garnish
	nonfat whipped topping for garnish

Lightly coat a mold with the cooking spray. In a saucepan, combine the lime juice, ½ cup water and sugar. Bring to a gentle boil, stirring until the sugar has dissolved. Boil rapidly for 2 minutes longer. Set aside. In a small saucepan, combine all of the berries with the 5 tablespoons of water. Bring to a boil. Reduce heat and simmer, covered, until the berries are soft. In a food processor, purée the berries. Strain through a sieve into a large mixing bowl to remove the seeds and skin. Set aside to cool. In a bowl, beat the egg whites until stiff but not dry. Pour in the sugar syrup in a steady stream, beating constantly. Fold in the berry purée and whipped topping. Pour the mixture into the mold. Freeze, covered, overnight. To serve, dip the bottom of the mold into hot water for approximately 10 seconds. Place a serving plate over the top of the mold, invert and shake to turn out. Garnish with lime slices and whipped topping.

FRUIT PASTRIES

(Makes 12/Serves 12)

Pastry:

4	cups all-purpose flour
2	tablespoons sugar
3	tablespoons solid vegetable shortening
	ice water
	non-stick cooking spray
1	egg white
2	tablespoons water

Prep Time: 45 minutes
Cook Time: 25-30 minutes

Nutritional Analysis
per serving

Calories	184
Fat	3 g
Sodium	4 mg
Protein	4 g
Carbohydrates	34 g
Cholesterol	0 mg

Preheat oven to 325°. In a bowl, mix the flour, sugar and shortening with a fork or pastry cutter until coarse. Gradually add enough ice water to form a soft dough. Turn the dough out onto a floured surface and roll to ¼-inch thickness with a floured rolling pin. Cut into twelve 4-inch circles. Lightly coat a large baking sheet with the cooking spray. Position the dough circles on top. In a bowl, mix the egg white with 2 tablespoons of water. Set aside.

Filling:

3	cups sliced peaches
16	ounces nonfat cream cheese, softened
2	tablespoons confectioners' sugar

Place a thin slice of fruit and an even amount of cream cheese on the lower half of each pastry circle. Fold the upper half of the pastry over and seal the edge well. Press the edges decoratively with the tines of a fork. Brush the tops with the egg white and water mixture. Bake, uncovered, for approximately 25 to 30 minutes or until golden. If the bottoms begin to brown before the tops, move the baking sheet to a higher oven rack. Dust the pastries with the confectioners' sugar.

Substitute other fruits for variety — apples, apricots, pitted cherries, etc.

Ginger Lime Sorbet

(Serves 6)

Prep Time: 35 minutes
Misc Time: Chill 25-30 minutes

Nutritional Analysis
per serving

Calories   94
Fat   0 g
Sodium   9 mg
Protein   1 g
Carbohydrates   23 g
Cholesterol   0 mg

³/₄	cup freshly squeezed lime juice
1	cup Simple Syrup, cooled (see page 101)
2	tablespoons confectioners' sugar
1	egg white
1½	teaspoons ground ginger
	crystallized ginger for garnish
	lime slices for garnish

In the chilled bowl of an electric ice cream maker, combine the lime juice and syrup. Churn for 15 minutes or until the ingredients have reached a slushy consistency. In a separate bowl, combine the confectioners' sugar and egg white. Beat until stiff. Spoon into the ice cream maker. Add the ginger. Churn for approximately 15 minutes longer or until the consistency of frozen yogurt. Transfer to a freezer container and freeze until ready for use. Garnish with crystallized ginger and a slice of lime.

Facing page — International Cuisine (pictured clockwise): Bouillabaisse, Roast Turkey, Paella Valenciana, Chicken Shish Kabobs, Pasta Puttanesca

SPECIAL NOTES

ABOUT THE AUTHOR

In her first book, Chris Borges makes international cooking a reality here at home. Through her travels, Chris received instruction from chefs all over the world in their native cuisines. Coupled with her research on healthy cooking, she adapted the more traditional international presentations to a lighter style, more in keeping with the needs of her own family as well as increasing popular demand. Her ability to combine the right ingredients in simple, easy-to-understand language, will make *International Light Cuisine* a welcome addition to any kitchen. Chris is currently working on her second book, *Tropical Light,* a lowfat, low cholesterol adaptation of recipes from Brazil, the Caribbean, Key West and other exotic ports of call.

Proceeds from the books will benefit a variety of community organizations with whom the author remains active. Chris is married with two sons and resides in St. Petersburg, Florida.

ILC Quarterly

Want more of the same terrific recipes and great suggestions for cooking light and healthy? It's yours for the asking in our newsletter, *ILC Quarterly.* Enjoy wonderful new recipes, more helpful hints and expanded information on nutrition, entertaining, exercise and even a special column dedicated to kids and cuisine.

To order, simply check the box on the *International Light Cuisine* Order Form. There's absolutely no purchase necessary. So hurry, send for your FREE copy of *ILC Quarterly* today.

Chris encourages your comments and questions. Write to her at:
c/o GemServ, Inc., Publisher
10460 Roosevelt Blvd, Suite 248
St. Petersburg, FL 33716-3818

INDEX

ALPHABETICAL

INDEX

INDEX

ORDER FORM

Purchaser's Name _____

Company Name (if any) _____

Address _____

City _____ State _____ Zip _____

Daytime Phone (___) _____ How many books shipped to this address? _____

Send gift to: (only if different from purchaser)

Name _____

Company Name (if any) _____

Address _____

City _____ State _____ Zip _____

Daytime Phone (___) _____ How many books shipped to this address? _____

For additional gift orders, please attach a separate sheet of paper.

❏ Gift wrap ($4.00 each)   ❏ Enclose gift card to read _____

- -

Please send ____ copies of *International Light Cuisine at $24.95 ea.* _____

Method of payment:
❏ Check or money order
❏ Visa   ❏ Mastercard
Card No. _ _ _ _ / _ _ _ _ / _ _ _ _ / _ _ _ _
Expiration Date _____ / _____
              month   year

Cardholder Signature _____
(required to process charge orders)

MAIL TO:
GemServ, Inc.
10460 Roosevelt Blvd., Suite 248
St. Petersburg, FL 33716-3818

Or FAX TO: (813) 573-0308

Florida residents add 7% sales tax on book(s) only	_____
Shipping/Handling on First book only 3.95	**$3.95**
Add'l books $2.50 ea.	_____
UPS 2nd Day $5.50 ea.	_____
Total order	_____

Make check payable to GemServ, Inc.

❏ Please rush my ***free*** copy of *ILC Quarterly*, your newsletter with more recipes, tips and trends on cooking for a healthy lifestyle.

Shipping: We will process and ship your order promptly via UPS Ground Service.
Second day service is available for an additional $5.50 per book. (Continental U.S. only)

ORDER FORM

Purchaser's Name _____

Company Name (if any) _____

Address _____

City _____ State _____ Zip _____

Daytime Phone (___) _____ How many books shipped to this address? _____

Send gift to: (only if different from purchaser)

Name _____

Company Name (if any) _____

Address _____

City _____ State _____ Zip _____

Daytime Phone (___) _____ How many books shipped to this address? _____

For additional gift orders, please attach a separate sheet of paper.

❏ Gift wrap ($4.00 each)   ❏ Enclose gift card to read _____

Please send _____ copies of *International Light Cuisine* at $24.95 ea. _____

Method of payment:

❏ Check or money order
❏ Visa   ❏ Mastercard

Card No. _ _ _ _ / _ _ _ _ / _ _ _ _ / _ _ _ _

Expiration Date _____ / _____
              month   year

Cardholder Signature _____
              (required to process charge orders)

MAIL TO:
GemServ, Inc.
10460 Roosevelt Blvd., Suite 248
St. Petersburg, FL 33716-3818

Or FAX TO: (813) 573-0308

Florida residents add 7% sales tax on book(s) only	_____
Shipping/Handling on First book only 3.95	**$3.95**
Add'l books $2.50 ea.	_____
UPS 2nd Day $5.50 ea.	_____
Total order	_____

Make check payable to GemServ, Inc.

❏ Please rush my *free* copy of *ILC Quarterly*, your newsletter with more recipes, tips and trends on cooking for a healthy lifestyle.

Shipping: We will process and ship your order promptly via UPS Ground Service. Second day service is available for an additional $5.50 per book. (Continental U.S. only)